UNDERSTANDING YOUR CAT

Books by Dr. Michael W. Fox

Inhumane Society: The American Way of Exploiting Animals
Superdog
The New Eden
Agricide: The Hidden Crisis That Affects Us All
The New Animal Doctor's Answer Book
The Whistling Hunters
Behavior of Wolves, Dogs, and Related Canids
One Earth, One Mind
Farm Animals; Husbandry, Behavior and Veterinary Practice
The Healing Touch
Dr. Michael Fox's Massage Program for Cats and Dogs
Love is a Happy Cat
How to Be Your Pet's Best Friend
Returning to Eden: Animal Rights and Human Responsibility
The Soul of the Wolf
Understanding Your Pet
Between Animal and Man: The Key to the Kingdom
Understanding Your Dog
Understanding Your Cat
Concepts in Ethology, Animal and Human Behavior
Integrative Development of Brain and Behavior in the Dog

Books Edited by Dr. Michael W. Fox

The Wild Canids
On The Fifth Day: Animal Rights and Human Ethics
The Dog: Its Domestication and Behavior
Readings in Ethology and Comparative Psychology
Abnormal Behavior in Animals
Advances in Animal Welfare Science

Children's Books

Animals Have Rights Too
The Way of the Dolphin
The Touchlings
Lessons From Nature: Fox's Fables
Whitepaws: A Coyote-Dog
Wild Dogs Three
What Is Your Dog Saying?
Ramu and Chennai
Sundance Coyote
The Wolf
Vixie, The Story of a Little Fox

UNDERSTANDING YOUR CAT

Dr. Michael W. Fox
D.Sc., Ph.D., MRCVS

St. Martin's Press
New York

Library of Congress Cataloging-in-Publication Data

Fox, Michael W.
    Understanding your cat / Michael W. Fox.
        p.   cm.
    ISBN 0-312-07107-8 (pbk.)
    1. Cats—Behavior.   2. Cats—Psychology.   3. Cats.   I. Title.
SF446.5.F68   1992
636.8'0887—dc20   91-39315
                                                                    CIP

First published in the United States by Coward, McCann & Geoghegan, Inc.

First U.S. Paperback Edition
10   9   8   7   6   5   4   3   2   1

For those who choose to walk alone.

Acknowledgments

The author acknowledges the help of many scientific colleagues who provided valuable references on cat behavior,* and is particularly grateful to Professor Paul Leyhausen, Max Planck Institut, Wuppertal, West Germany, much of whose published scientific work is reviewed in this book. Some of the material in Chapter 9 has been published, in part, in my column *"Ask the Vet"* in *Family Health* magazine. He is also grateful to Patricia Brehaut Soliman, Editor, for constructive criticism in the preparation of the manuscript.

*For a comprehensive bibliography see Fox, 1974, in references.

Contents

Foreword

MY FIRST REACTION to the thought of writing *Understanding Your Cat* was, How can I be so arrogant as to presume to know anything about such a distant and inscrutable being? I was encouraged, though, by two things: First, my own research on behavior development in cats (and their distant relatives, dogs, wolves, and foxes) showed how the subtle behavior of the cat unfolds. The second spur was my awareness of the legion of cat owners and my conviction that their relationships with their pets could be enriched and even improved if some information on cat behavior and psychology were available. I have a library of cat books, and all of them are like brown paper sandwiches: no substance. I wasn't looking for pretty pictures, cute anecdotes, or tedious lists of breed characteristics. Instead, I wanted substance— facts about how cats communicate; what kinds of relationships they have with each other; what their brains, senses, and intelligence are like compared to dogs and man. What concerned me were questions like, What is the best way to raise and socialize a kitten? Why are cats so aloof compared to dogs, so hard to train and yet at times so sensitive and aware that they seem to possess a power akin to ESP? Is the cat really domesticated and how does it fit into our modern way of life? Does the cat suffer any of the neuroses and psychoses we see in man that have been reported in the dog?

This book deals with such questions and provides answers for these and many others. It has been exciting for me to sleuth through many scientific studies of the cat which are buried in esoteric journals—lost to those who have neither the access nor the time for such pursuits.

The incredible and fascinating facts about the cat reported in this book give flesh to our understanding of the psyche and behavior of this remarkable animal. And a deeper understanding of cats can lead to a greater awareness and appreciation of all living things, as well as to an understanding of our own nature, which the cat reflects in many ways.

Introduction

It gives me great pleasure to write an introduction to this reissue of *Understanding Your Cat,* since it has already helped one generation of cat owners and several generations of cats from the time that it was first published in 1974.

Animals are a constant in our lives and they do not change from one generation to the next. But language does change, so the reader should forgive such outdated "sexist" overtones as my use of the term man and mankind, instead of people and humanity. However, in spite of changes in word usage and in our attitudes and values, the facts about cat behavior in this book remain unchanged because cats, more ancient than we, will always be cats.

As a veterinarian, I feel that this book makes a significant contribution to helping improve the health and well-being of our feline companions. This is because the better we understand them, the better we can care for them. Love without understanding is not enough.

As an animal behaviorist (or ethologist) and as an advocate of animals rights and protection, I am convinced that progress in the humane treatment of animals comes first, not through laws, but through a change in our attitudes and values through understanding animals' behavior, development, social and emotional needs. Such understanding leads to a greater respect and reverence for all creatures and a deeper communion with all of creation.

It also means a more fulfilling relationship with our animal companions and to this end, I dedicate my book.

—DR. MICHAEL W. FOX
Washington, D.C., 1991

UNDERSTANDING YOUR CAT

1

Man and Cat

SHE LIES BY the fire, so close she must be scorching, with her eyes almost closed. The fire crackles and spurts flame and she flicks an ear and rolls over, basking in the warmth of the hearth. Could this be the same cat who that morning was a gray shadow in the silver dawn—that moved in silence, that somehow had no form because it became invisible when it didn't move? Could this cat, savoring the luxuries of the home—well-fed, warm, loved, and totally indulged—be the same creature of the shadows that in an instant could pounce and kill an unwary bird, mouse, or rabbit in the fields of morning dew?

The domestic cat enjoys the fruits of two worlds, the captive and the wild. The cat is an opportunist, some say, while others feel that man did not domesticate the cat but rather the reverse. To be so flexible and adaptable the cat must surely possess some intelligence or capacity lacking in most people.

We are either fully domesticated (and neurotic) urbanites or quasi-free-living country folk who still need many of the accoutrements of civilization. We are overcivilized and dependent upon it: The cat is civil and has the advantage over us in that it enjoys the fruits of our world and of its own, which no man can tame. The "domestic" cat, then, is a unique creature, which lives between two worlds. The imprint of man upon the cat, unlike the dog, has had little influence on its choice.

From archaeological remains it is evident that the dog was domesticated much earlier than the cat. The first cats to be domesticated were those of the Egyptians. The general consensus is that the Kaffir cat *(Felis libica)* * is the main progenitor of the domesticated cat *(Felis domestica)*. It can be easily tamed and will crossbreed with the domestic cat and produce fertile offspring. It is about the size of a large domestic cat (see Figure 1) and has a short, yellow-buff coat with faint horizontal bands on the tail and legs and occasionally on the body.

Because the domestic cat is now widespread throughout Europe it was once thought that the European wildcat *(Felis sylvestris)* was a likely ancestor. This cat, which is much larger and stockier than the domestic cat, is extremely wild, and even when bottle-raised the young are virtually intractable. Although it will hybridize with the domestic cat, its offspring are reportedly weak and often infertile. There are also structural differences in the skull of the wildcat which set it apart from the domestic cat and further rule out the possibility that any of its genes might have contributed to the makeup of contemporary cats.

In ancient Egypt, cats were part of the culture as early as

---

* Many regional varieties or subspecies of *Felis libica* have been identified. These include the Kaffir, or cape, cat, the steppe cat, the Libyan, or fettered, cat, and the Indian desert cat. Altogether there are twelve races, ranging from Mediterranean islands (Majorca, Corsica, Sardinia, Crete) and North Africa to Turkestan and India.

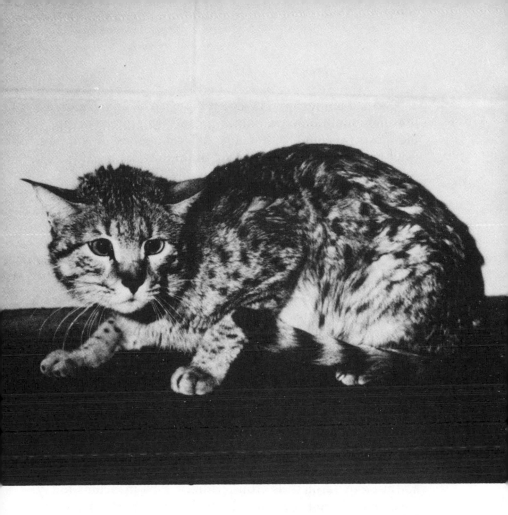

Figure 1. The Kaffir, or Cape cat, *Felis libica,* wild ancestor of the domestic cat

2500 B.C., if not earlier. They were depicted clearly in papyrus drawings, tomb frescoes, paintings, and sculpture. The Egyptians experimented with many different kinds of animals, even hyenas, as they developed an agriculture and domesticated livestock. The cats were possibly first introduced from Libya or Nubia and their usefulness was soon realized by the Egyptians. There was no better animal to control the rat that plagued their granaries. The cat of Egypt was also trained to help hunt and retrieve wild birds along the Nile and even to fish for its master. Ultimately the cat was to attain a high position in the religion of this advanced culture, being represented in the form of Bastet, the cat-headed goddess, symbol of femininity, grace, and fertility. The Greek historian Herodotus recorded the reverence paid the domestic cats of the Egyptians. When a housecat died, members of the household were required by law to shave off their eyebrows as a sign of mourning. On one occasion, a Roman soldier was killed by an inflamed mob of Egyptians for killing a cat.

The extent to which the Egyptians venerated the cat is perhaps best exemplified by the excavation, a century ago, at Beni Hassan, which revealed more than 300,000 mummified cats. Nineteen tons of these remains were shipped to England and used by farmers as crop fertilizer! Few museums today have any of these specimens, which could have offered invaluable clues to the ancestry of the modern domestic cat. Recently, however, Dr. T. C. S. Morrison-Scott of the British Museum of Natural History, London, studied 190 skulls, dated between 600 and 200 B.C., from an excavation at Gizeh. All but three specimens resembled the Kaffir cat, *Felis libica;* the other three coincidental specimens were of the jungle cat, *Felis chaus.*

There are, however, no historical records of when the first tame cats came to Europe. Possibly the Phoenician

Figure 2. Mummified cats from ancient Egypt. The cat was revered and buried ceremonially by the worshipers of Bastet, the cat goddess.

traders brought cats in their ships as they explored and developed trade in European ports. Legend has it that the Egyptians so highly venerated their cats that their exportation was forbidden; Phoenician traders may have engaged in a lucrative smuggling business and were most likely responsible for the cat's dissemination from its Egyptian cradle of origin. By 1000 B.C. the cat was known in China and later in Japan, where it served an invaluable role in the silkworm industry, protecting cocoons from rats. Cats were also used in temples and monasteries to protect priceless manuscripts from the destructive appetites and curiosity of the rat.

Some hold that the domestic cat was first introduced in England when the Phoenicians visited the Cornish tin mines in the island's southwest. Others believe that the Romans were responsible, not only for bringing the ancient Britons out of the Stone Age, but also for civilizing them by introducing the domestic cat into their lives!

As the cultures of various European countries developed, so the cat became something more than a controller of vermin. It became part of the culture itself, as exemplified by the many superstitions and practices that evolved and revolved around it. For example, if a cat sneezed, it was going to rain soon; to make a building sound, it was necessary, while it was being constructed, to seal a cat in the wall. In many countries, burying a cat or kitten alive would ensure a good harvest. So cats themselves often fell victim to their own reputation. They were sacrificed, frequently by being burned alive, to "cure" an epidemic or other misfortune that had befallen some community. For instance, in France, for more than three hundred years, cats were burned in a cage over a fire on the Eve of St. John's.

While settlements and cities continued to develop, so did the rat population. Wherever man went and prospered, likewise did the rat. It followed in the wake of historic invasions, voyages of exploration, and, later, commercial trade routes. Not only did they devastate the grain stores of agrarian societies, and so contribute to famine, but they also brought disease: the plague of the Philistines in 1070 B.C.; the plague of the Middle East in 430 B.C.; the worst was the Black Death that ravaged Europe and Asia, killing millions of people in the mid-fourteenth century. Half the population of London died in the 1660's from bubonic plague. (And other epidemics since have decimated human populations in many parts of the world.)

As man's only ally against the rat, the cat rose in esteem and value in the Middle Ages. But in spite of this, the church turned against it because many people followed occult and pagan practices that were outlawed. Since many of these "black arts" included cats in their rituals, cats, too, were persecuted. The pagan cult of Freyia, for example, was a witch-cult that venerated and identified with the fertility and mystique of the cat. In the fifteenth century, Pope Innocent VIII, in order to protect the interests of the Catholic church by stamping out the practice of witchcraft, encouraged the destruction of cats, which came to be regarded as powerful allies of witches. Witch-hunt also came to mean cat-hunt. The cats of suspects, often innocent old recluses or nonconformist eccentrics the paranoid village folk feared, were caught and burned or drowned, sometimes along with their owners. Punishment for sheltering a cat or caring for a sick cat could range from torture to burning at the stake.

As a consequence of this religious-political regime of the Middle Ages, which was bent on maintaining its supremacy over other cults and religions, the cat became a symbol of evil. Anyone owning a cat might be suspect, and so the cat fell into dark disrepute in Europe in the Middle Ages. Accusations of witchcraft involving cats were not limited to Europe; they also led to many deaths in South Carolina and New England in America.

This persecution of the cat was slow to wane since the negative attitude it created in the people toward cats endured. Human attitudes are notoriously difficult to change; they are passed on from parent to child, and even today prejudice of many kinds limits human experience and interaction. Some people still see cats as sinister and distant or evil and unpredictable, and they project their fears onto the cat, who may well pick up these bad vibrations. A child may acquire these same attitudes from the parents and never be free to see the cat for what it really is.

The negative attitude toward the cat in the Middle Ages endured for many generations, but the turning point came in the eighteenth century. What changed the relationship between man and cat was the invasion of Europe by the brown rat. This voracious animal, almost as versatile and adaptable as man himself, swept across Europe from the east and soon ousted the indigenous black rat. A new respect grew for the cat since it was man's sole ally against the invader. In many places—homes, bakeries, and other places where foodstuffs were stored or prepared—poison baits were too hazardous to be used to control the rats. A good ratting cat brought a high price. Even today in Europe, no one thinks twice when they see a sleeping cat in a bakery window, surrounded by fresh-baked loaves and pastries. It is accepted as a clean animal that will keep the establishment vermin-free.

And so a new respect grew for the cat, who once again was recognized and appreciated as an invaluable ally against the rat. Cats were deployed as rat-catchers in buildings—post offices, warehouses, stores, and barracks—where it could at least hold down the rat populations to some extent. With the "age of enlightenment" the negative attitude to cats changed profoundly. In his book on the cat Fernand Méry makes an important point relevant to this dramatic mood shift after the long persecution of the Middle Ages. In the nineteenth century Pasteur revealed that microbes were the cause of many diseases and were directly associated with dirt and squalor. Zoophobia flourished. People simply avoided touching any animal that smelled—dogs were shunned and horses touched only by a gloved hand. (Such paranoia still exists today in America, where many people keep no animal in the house because they feel that animals are unsanitary and can infect them with worms, rabies, and other diseases!) But the cat is a fastidiously clean animal, forever washing itself and usually scrupulous about its toilet. And so the cat was the *one* animal most people felt they could safely keep in the house and caress without fear of infection. Méry concludes that people, deprived of close interaction with other animals because of this fear of contagious disease, opened their homes to the cat and gave it the place in their hearts that it never could have experienced as a mere servant controlling rats. People began to care for the cat, admire and understand it, and see it for what it was. So often a common crisis brings us together, temporarily or permanently eliminating fear and prejudice. So it was with cats and people, thanks to the brown rat and Pasteur's discovery of the microbe.

Today, people of the Western hemisphere have a more realistic attitude toward cats and animals in general, although some myths and phobias persist. One is that a cat will choke a baby in trying to lick milk out of its throat and that it is bad luck to have a black cat cross your path (although in England it's good luck—but bad luck if you meet a white cat!). In America, in contrast to European standards, we have perhaps gone overboard in our hygiene fetish. I see a return to the attitudes generated by Pasteur's discoveries in our disease-conscious, health-oriented, vitamin-supplemented culture. A cat in a delicatessen window would soon be evicted by the Board of Health or the establishment would be closed! No cats or dogs in restaurants or grocery stores; perhaps children will be banned next! In Europe today it is a common sight to see a well-mannered dog sitting by its owner's table in a fashionable restaurant or a cat out shopping on its owner's shoulder at the local grocery. In Europe people share more of their lives with their pets, and much of this I attribute to a difference in attitude vis-à-vis cleanliness and disease. I will have more to say about contemporary relationships between man and cat later in this book; the history of the cat in America has not yet been discussed.

Dr. Neil Todd of the Carnivore Genetics Research Center in Newtonville, Massachusetts, believes that the domestic cat was not introduced into northeastern North America until the seventeenth century (possibly to combat the rat problem that erupted in cities like Philadelphia). The original populations brought to the United States and to New Zealand and Australia one hundred and fifty years later were principally from England (and to a lesser extent from the Netherlands). Todd has found, after studying the frequencies of occurrence of various coat colors in cat populations throughout the world, that it is possible to age a given population. The genetic character of a local cat population (which is reflected in various coat colors) is apparently fixed and stabilized and is very similar to what a random sampling of the coat colors of a parent population would reveal. Dark-colored cats are more frequently seen in cities, and it follows that the greatest change in gene frequencies of coat color have occurred in Europe as a consequence of earlier urbanization than in colonial populations. Cats studied in various cities of the northeast United States approximate a sample of English cats of the mid-seventeenth century. Cats of eastern Australia represent another sample, made in the early nineteenth century. Thus the random assortment of cats brought over by the early settlers simply ceased to evolve at the same pace as their urbanizing relatives in Europe, who continued to change. The latter developed a greater range of dark-colored coats, while the cats imported to the New World tended to remain unchanged for generations.

Today the cat is very much part of our lives, and in spite of the changes in human attitudes and values and in the structure of society itself since the industrial revolution, the domestic cat remains unchanged. It is aloof, it endures, its very essence seeming immune to the chaotic forces of an evolving, struggling humanity that surrounds it. The cat's detached, calculated indifference, its equipoise—resting but alert to seize an opportunity that is to its advantage—its nonstriving, its affectionate but unconditional giving, its freedom from dependencies and "shouldisms," are attributes devoutly to be wished! This very nature of the cat sets it apart from all other animals that man has domesticated or attempted to domesticate. Often referred to as "she," because we still project a female grace-fertility archetype onto the animal, the cat has entered into the hearts and minds of many people as perhaps no other domestic animal has. No animal has such a history of veneration and fear, and although man has been close to the cat for so long, it is perhaps one of the least understood of the animals that have been in close association with man for so long. Has familiarity bred indifference or contempt, or does the awe, the mystery and folklore surrounding the cat prevent us from seeing it and appreciating the cat for what it is?

A closer look at its cousins—lions, cheetahs, and numerous smaller wildcats—could give us a clearer picture of the nature of the cat and of its evolution before man intervened in its destiny.

2

Wildcat Relatives

WHEN I FIRST started studying cats, I thought it would be an easy matter to review the different species and get a more global picture of the felid family. How wrong I was. There are dozens of different species throughout the world, and little is known about their social behavior and ecology since few naturalistic studies have been done. One of the major reasons for this is that all cats, with the exception of the lion, live a solitary life, and to follow a cat not much larger than a housecat through the jungles of South America or Asia is an impossible task.

Some species are so similar that experts still argue which is which. But they will probably not be contending for much longer since many of these cat species are on the road to extinction. The small spotted cats from South America have been hunted relentlessly for their skins for decades, and now public demand for live specimens to keep as pets contributes to continued depredation. Countless numbers die in transit or while being held by native trappers before shipment. The fur trade is also contributing to the extinction of the larger cats—tigers, leopards, and cheetahs—as well as the smaller cats—ocelots and margays. And poaching and illegal dealings in high political places in the countries where these animals live continually threaten their survival. It is essential to arrest this tide of depredation, to save not only the cats but also the places where they live. Such ecosystems will be destroyed if native predators, like the cat, are eliminated. These hunters are called the apex predators because they are at the top of the food chain. Plants trap solar energy which is converted into organic nutrients for herbivores, the plant-eating animals. These, in turn, provide the staple diet for the flesh-eating predators. Any break in this chain—the use of herbicides, insecticides, or killing off most of the predators—can upset the balance of nature and the ecosystem collapses. Suppose the predators became extinct. There would be no population control of the plant-eaters, who produce excess young in an adaptive "anticipation" of being preyed upon. With no control of their numbers, the plant-eaters would overgraze, destroy the plant life and ultimately starve to death. In India, for instance, where there are fewer than 2,000 tigers in the wild, attempts are being made to save this endangered "national treasure." Hard-core economic and social issues have to be faced though. How much space (*i.e.,* home range size) does one tiger need? If food is plentiful, 50 square miles might do. To set aside a sanctuary of 500 square miles is politically and economically difficult when the land is sorely needed by an expanding human population. A sanctuary that size might support ten or so tigers, but is that enough tigers to form a good gene pool essential to the continuation of the species?

We don't know and it might be too late. The answer in many cases may be to develop highly manned artificial mini-ecologies where food is provided and every plant, animal, parasite, and disease is carefully monitored. Will this be the "wilderness" that our children's children will inherit?

At the time of this writing, my friend Dr. George Schaller of the New York Zoological Society is studying the snow leopard in the Himalayas, and Dr. Pete Berrie, Field Biologist, the University of Georgia, is appraising the status of the small cats in Paraguay. Both are using one of the advances of space technology: the biotelemeter. A minute transmitter is attached to a collar which is fastened around the animal's neck after it has been caught. After its release, it is a relatively easy task to follow the subject, map out its home range, and even get close enough sometimes to observe it. This is the only feasible way of studying such elusive, solitary hunters. It is to be hoped that the knowledge of such dedicated ecologists will help in setting up good management programs which will aid in the conservation, not only of these cats, but of the whole ecosystem or environment of which they are an integral part.

Although it is necessary, albeit painful, to look into the future this way, archaeologists and paleontologists have opened a fascinating door into the past which gives us a picture of where the cats came from. (Where they are going now is man's responsibility.)

Fossil cats can be traced as far back as thirty-five million years. It is believed that the first cats descended from the same common origin as civets and mongooses (see Figure 3). There were two branches in the cat's evolution in this group of carnivorous (flesh-eating) mammals. One branch was doomed to extinction. This was the saber-toothed cats which, exemplified by the saber-toothed tiger, were well adapted for killing mastodons, mammoths, and elephants. Their extinc-

31

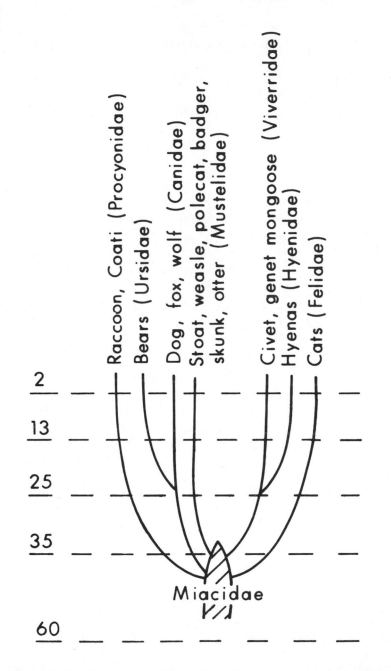

Figure 3. Evolutionary chart showing origin of the cat family and its relationship with other carnivores. Millions of years of evolution are shown on the left of the diagram

tion has been partially attributed to a more successful hunter of these large mammoths. Man. For thousands of years, long before man evolved an agricultural way of life and began to domesticate farm animals, dogs, and cats, he was a hunter. He became an integral part of the ecosystem and this fact is evident today in Africa, one of the last continents where man is a hunter. Stop the hunting and the ecological imbalance follows. Stop wolves from killing deer and the deer become too numerous; they kill the vegetation by overgrazing and eventually die of starvation. Stop native hunters from killing big game, especially elephants, and the same thing happens. In many parts of Africa today, elephants are "protected" from native hunters and this unwise practice is rapidly destroying the habitat since there are too many elephants. Their numbers were regulated before man came onto the scene, by the saber-toothed cats.

While this saber-toothed branch of the cat family became extinct, the other branch endured. There is one cat living today that most closely resembles these extinct saber-toothed cats. This is the clouded leopard from Southeast Asia, which has the largest canine teeth in proportion to its body of all the cat family (see Figure 4).

Wildcats are to be found both in the Old and the New Worlds. They generally prefer warm climates, although the lynx in Europe and North America, the bobcat in North America, and the snow leopard in the Himalayas are adapted to much colder climates. Cats of the Old World include the leopard, tiger, lion, and cheetah (and the black form also known as the panther), and a number of smaller cats. One of the most handsome is the caracal, a leaner version of the lynx, which replaces the lynx in warm regions of the Old World.

Cats were absent in South America until the Panama land bridge, connecting North and South America, was reestablished some five million years ago. The jaguar, ocelot,

Asian black leopard

Persian leopard

Snow leopard from the Himalayas

Figure 4. SOME OF THE LARGER MEMBERS OF THE CAT FAMILY

Clouded leopard from Southeast Asia

puma, and a number of smaller cats (like the jaguarundi, margay, pampas cat, and little spotted cat) are exclusive to the New World. The lynx is the only cat found in both the New and the Old Worlds. The South American variety of puma is much smaller than its North American counterpart, the latter often being referred to as the mountain lion, cougar, or catamount.

The most abundant source of wildcats is Asia, but, interestingly, in spite of ideal conditions, no cats are native to the West Indies, Madagascar, Australia, and the Oceania Islands.

For classification purposes, the cat family *(Felidae)* is divided into three subfamilies, or genera. The first, *Felis,* includes: domestic cat, European wildcat; from *Africa and Asia:* Kaffir cat, sand cat, jungle cat; from *Africa:* black-footed cat, caracal (African lynx), serval, golden cat; from *Asia:* Pallas's cat, marbled cat, Chinese desert cat, Temminck's golden cat, leopard cat, rusty-spotted cat, fishing cat, flatheaded cat, Bornean red cat, clouded leopard; from *North America, Canada, and Northern Europe:* lynx; North America: bobcat; North and South America: puma, jaguarundi; from *South America:* Geoffroy's cat, little spotted cat, kodkod, margay, ocelot, pampas cat, Andean cat.

The second genus *(Panthera)* consists of the larger cats; from *Asia:* the snow leopard and tiger; *Africa and India:* the lion, leopard, or panther; *South America:* the jaguar.

In the third genus *(Acinonyx)* is the cheetah of Africa and Iran, now extinct in Asia.

Many of these wildcats will interbreed. Hybrids of lion and tiger ("tiglons") are quite common in zoos. Many of the cats show color mutations, white (albinism) being rare, as in the white tigers of India. Melanism (black coat) is more common, as in the jungle cat and Geoffroy's cat (see Figure 6). Several of the smaller cat species will also interbreed. Domestic cats

36

have been crossed with lynx, leopard cat, jungle cat, kaffir cat, and European wildcat. Unfortunately, no details of the behavior and development of these interesting hybrids were reported.

Most of these small cat species look very appealing, and many find their way into pet stores, but to buy one as a pet is to help in their destruction. It is a rationalization to say, well, it's in the pet store and it can't be sent back so I might as well have it. You buy it and the pet store orders more for likeminded buyers. All states should pass laws barring the sale of endangered species and *no wild animals should be sold as pets*—even raccoons and opossums. They do *not* make good pets, no matter how cute and friendly they seem as infants. Since these animals are basically solitary species, as they mature, the tie with mother is broken. It does not persist as a social bond as it does in the social mammals such as dogs or wolves. With maturity they will fight restraint, defy discipline, and determinedly seek their own independence. There are exceptions: Some adult margays and ocelots are quite tractable, but for the one that survives in the house, perhaps four or six have died while being caught, impounded, and shipped.

With the exception of the lion and cheetah, all wild cats use the same specialized method of hunting. They are solitary, using concealment and strategies of stealth and ambush to get close enough to be able to rush, leap at, and pull down their prey. They are not built to course after their prey like wolves and wild dogs. Their retractile claws are used to hold the prey so they can quickly position themselves for the killing bite, which is aimed at the back of the neck. The long canine teeth are used to sever the spinal cord of the prey. The incredible accuracy of this coup de grace and the development of prey-killing behavior in the domestic cat will be discussed in detail in Chapter 5. Some of these wild cats may be seen hunting in

Jaguarundi

Figure 5. A Variety of Cats Are Found in South America

Pampas cat

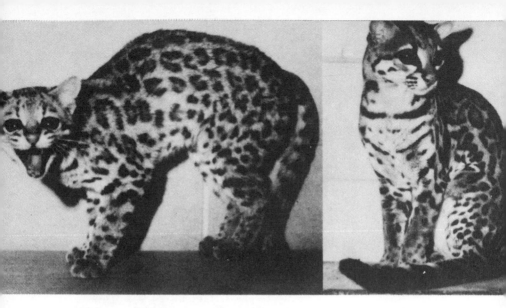

Little spotted cat   Margay

Ocelot (a tiger-striped variant)

Armur leopard cat from East Asia and Japan

European wildcat

Jungle cat from India,
Iran, and Egypt

Figure 6. ALL THESE WILD CATS HAVE BEEN ONCE THOUGHT TO HAVE
CONTRIBUTED TO THE MAKEUP OF THE DOMESTICATED CAT

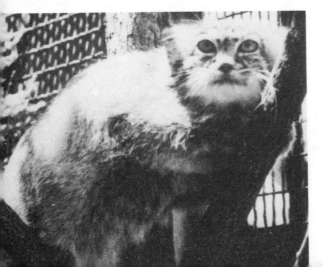

Pallas's cat from central Asia

Figure 7. From North America the lynx (above) and smaller bobcat (below) have ear and cheek tufts which enhance facial displays

The Leopard cat (above) and
Flat-headed cat (left) are two
intriguing species from Asia

The Sand cat comes from the deserts of North Africa

threes or fours. These are family groups, with mother taking her offspring on the hunt to "train" them before they are old enough to be independent (see Figure 8). The father never stays around to help her tend the young, although in captivity some paternalism may be seen.

Unlike the other cats, the cheetah is the only one to course after its prey: It is essentially the "dog" of the cat family. Its claws are not retractile, and since its canine teeth are relatively short, it usually strangles its prey by seizing it under the throat.

The lion is the "wolf" of the cat world since it is the only highly sociable species, living in "prides" that vary in size from region to region depending on how much food is available. Food became so scarce in North Africa that the now extinct Barbary lion was never seen in a pride—only singles and pairs were recorded. Clearly, the ecology (distribution and abundance of food) does influence sociability and the kind of social organization to a high degree.

The remarkable variation in size of the cats (see Figure 9) points to another rule of nature. The cats have evolved a body size adapted to the size of prey they especially like to hunt. In this way, several species of cats of varying size can live in the same region or habitat. Each has its own niche, or place, with the smallest hunting mice, lizards, and insects, and the larger ones ignoring such tidbits and instead focusing on larger prey, deer, gazelles, and other hoofed herbivores. With each species having its own special niche, there is no competition over the same prey.

It is intriguing that only the lion became highly sociable, gaining the advantage of a cooperative society in which individuals in the pride help one another to hunt. This offset the disadvantages of having to "belong" to a group, to forgo independence, and sometimes to suffer the privations of being low in the rank order. Each pride has its patriarch, the maned male who is ill-equipped for hunting, a task given to the lionesses. In some prides there may be two male overlords, but usually there is only one, and he evicts male cubs when they are about two years old. These young males leave their natal pride and embark on a solitary life of one or more years until they can build up a harem of young lionesses. A lone male may successfully lure a female away from her pride, although he is often repelled by the patriarch and high-ranking females of her family.

The lion spends much of the day sleeping and occasionally roaring and spraying to demark the pride's territory and movements. When his queens make a kill, he eats first. At the dinner table, lions have no manners! While Cape hunting dogs will sit back and let their cubs eat first, in the lion pride the strongest eat first. After the competitive feast is over, however, there is much head rubbing and face licking, as though to make up for things and to reaffirm their affection for each other.

Interestingly, the lions' table manners are not without purpose. Unlike any other wild cat, the lioness has a prolonged estrus, or heat period, during which she is receptive to the male to a degree unprecedented in the cat world. Dr. George Schaller, in his excellent book *The Serengeti Lion: A Study in Predatory-Prey Relations,* noted that copulations with a single patriarch may number more than one hundred and twenty per day. This high frequency of sexual intercourse is thought to keep the pride together, much in the same way as sex has a social function in the apes and man. Unfortunately, though, this does result in frequent births and so the check on the population occurs around the dinner table. Low-ranking females and cubs, especially in times when food is scarce, may suffer respectively from lowered fertility and abortion or die of starvation. The lionesses will take turns in allowing one

Figure 8. A Serengeti cheetah allows her two cubs to feed off her kill, a Thompson's gazelle. Soon the family will break up and the young will hunt for themselves

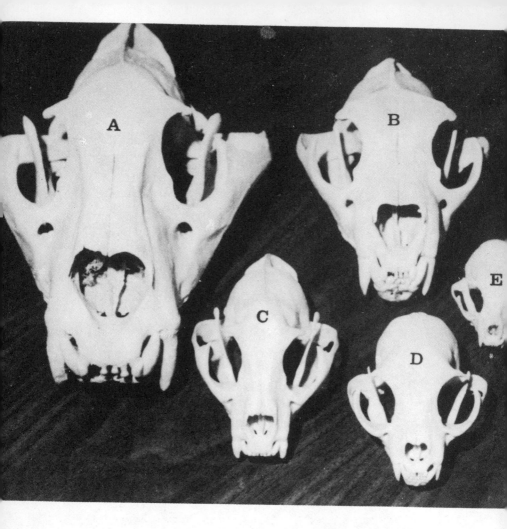

Figure 9. Skulls of various cat species exemplify the great range of size in this family of hunters adapted to a particular kind and size of prey: (a) Bengal tiger, (b) Snow leopard, (c) African Golden cat, (d) Bobcat, and (e) Jaguarundi

another's cubs to nurse, and this communal nursing—coupled with a great deal of reproductive sexual activity between the patriarch and mature lionesses, in the pride—would necessitate some method of "birth control." This is a fascinating story which I have outlined in some detail because we do tend to place human values on what we see animals doing and often, consequently, misjudge them. We might misjudge the lions for not allowing the cubs to eat first. If the lions did not have this rigid social order at a kill, the survival of the pride might be threatened. Other hunters control the population at different times. In the case of the wolf, control tends to be before the cubs are born, since the dominant female prevents others from mating. This is a "pre-copulation" birth control. The dominant female of a pack of Cape hunting dogs may kill the cubs of a lower-ranking female if she herself has a litter. Different species have evolved different methods of population control, but it cannot be regarded as conscious behavior but rather as an automatic mechanism (an instinct if you like) which is automatically switched on at certain times and in particular contexts.

Cats that live a solitary life become independent at an early age, spend only a short while with the mother, and have little time to learn much from the parent by observation and imitation. "Cultural traditions" passed on from one generation to the next concerning particular details about the parent's home range—where and what to hunt, where to drink, to seek shelter or refuge, which places and animals to avoid, and so on—would also be of little value. For the lion or wolf cub or young chimp, gorilla, baboon, and child of early man, this would be important. Infancy and dependency might be advantageously prolonged where the offspring stay with the family group and in their territory or range. For most cats, such learning is of little value since they are soon forced out of the parent's

Figure 10. The male lion of the pride seizes a cub with an inhibited neck bite, a sexual posture associated with dominance

The cub protests; note the obvious interest of other cubs in the pride

territory and have to find their own place elsewhere. A young cat may find unoccupied territory quite close to its mother's, and set up residence there.

Some solitaries, like the bobcat and leopard, rarely meet; instead they prefer to keep a distance and communicate vocally, marking the edge of their territories with scent from urine and feces. Possibly in order to avoid contact, they will move through their home ranges on a fairly fixed schedule. In one area studied, bobcats in different territories took several days to roam through their hunting ranges that tended to overlap. Chance encounters were minimized by the cats all moving in the same counter-clockwise pattern! (More will be said in Chapter 5 about how the domestic cat utilizes *its* home range to avoid encounters and what happens when it does confront another cat.) It is important then for the infant cat to mature rapidly and not to rely on others for its survival. Independence is facilitated by the young cat's being endowed with many innate actions or instincts. Although these do impose certain limits on the animal's capacity to develop new actions and explore new possibilities in its environment, they nonetheless insure that the little cat will be able to take care of itself at an early age.

Some of the cat's remarkable abilities and senses, which enable it not only to survive but to raise its young and protect them from larger predators who might make a meal of them, deserve our in-depth exploration.

3

Nine Senses for "Nine Lives"

THE OTHER NIGHT I was out studying a group of three wild dogs in a run-down part of St. Louis. There were four cats in the area and we had an excellent opportunity to observe them. Right on schedule at 11:30 P.M. an old black-and-white tomcat came out of his home for his nightly prowl. He stepped slowly and purposefully into the alley adjoining his backyard and immediately sensed my presence. His eyes flashed momentarily as my camera's strobe light caught him. Unperturbed, he strolled across the alley, sniffed a gatepost, then turned around, backed up, and sprayed. What made him do this and what did his senses tell him about the gatepost? Perhaps it was the olfactory "flag" he hoisted every night to inform other cats who might pass that he was out and about. Suddenly he froze in midstride, his ears pointing to a clump of thick weeds bursting out of an abandoned backyard. My senses told me nothing, except that the old tomcat was obviously onto something. Was it the ultrasonic squeak of a mouse, the rustling of a large roach, or the plump shadow of a rat that caught his eyes and filled his nose with the rich aroma of the underworld? Abruptly he turned and ran off into the shadows; moments later I discovered what had alarmed him. The three dogs that I was studying were coming out of the abandoned house, again on schedule at 11:50 P.M. The cat heard them long before I even saw them. Perhaps he anticipated their coming because he knew their time schedule, and knew, as well, that these hungry dogs were to be avoided. Although shy of people, they would make a meal of a cat if they ever succeeded in catching it.

Hunting and foraging together, these dogs were able to support one another; one would act as a lookout while the others were eating; one might sight a rat or squirrel and immediately alert its companions. Such mutual support increased the efficiency of each dog and essentially three brains, three noses, six ears, and six eyes were better than one or two of each. But the cat who hunts alone must rely totally on its own senses, which must be tuned for many cues—movement, sounds, and smells that could mean food or danger. And there must also be an efficient memory storage and recall system to account for all the many and varied stimuli in the animal's world. A cat has nine senses, seven of which will be discussed in this chapter. They include the senses of smell, taste, touch, temperature, balance, sight, and hearing. The other two, the senses of direction and time, will be discussed in the next chapter.

The cat has a highly evolved brain that, in terms of complexity, lies approximately midway between lower mammals (rats and mice) and the apes, the most highly developed mammals on the evolutionary scale. A great deal is known about the structure and function of the cat's nervous system because the cat, more than any other mammal, has been used extensively by scientists for many years.

The brain of the cat (see Figure 11) is basically the same as that of the human being, the main differences being that man has larger frontal lobes, memory association areas, and also a well-developed center for speech. These brain parts are in the neocortex, the most recently evolved part of the brain. The more primitive parts of the brain under this large bilobed structure are virtually identical in cat and man. The spinal cord conducts impulses to and from the brain to the extremities; the cerebellum, a convoluted structure at the base of the skull, is associated with movement, posture, and balance in both man and cat. Deep beneath the neocortex is the limbic system, the center of emotions and sensations—sex, rage, pain, pleasure, hunger, fear, and so on. It is not anthropomorphic to say that the cat experiences emotions as we do. It is logical to conclude that they do so since they have the same brain center for such feelings as we have.

Researchers have explored these areas in the cat in great detail. Stimulation of some brain sites with electrodes can turn a docile cat into a raging beast that will attack anything that comes near its cage. Stimulation of other regions, or destruction of certain areas, can inhibit or prevent such reactions. Minute amounts of drugs can be injected through micro-cannulas (fine hollow needles) inserted at specific brain sites in order to explore further the biochemistry of behavior, memory, and emotional reactions. Tiny pellets of hormones inserted in the right place can bring a castrated cat back to full sexual vigor. Such studies can lead us to a better understanding of how the infinitely complex brain operates. Without such knowledge we would not have the basic ground plan which today enables the neurosurgeon to correct a number of brain

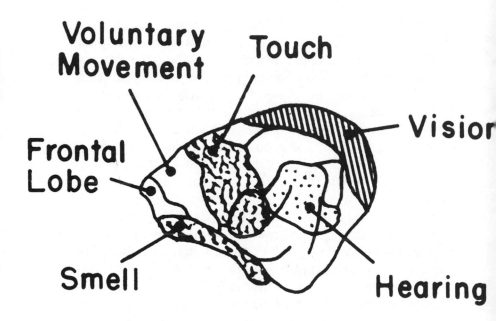

Figure 11. Schema of cat brain (neocortex) showing various regions which have specific functions

disorders in human beings. We can thank the cat for this. Many people, including myself, question the morality and ethics of using animals for such biomedical research. It is a fact, though, that had such animal studies never been done, our understanding of the human brain today would be negligible. We would also possess neither the knowledge nor the skills for corrective neurosurgery on human patients.

It is also a fact that cats (and other animals, too—rats, dogs, and monkeys) are "sacrificed" in many unnecessary experiments. The Animal Welfare Act of 1970 has done much to improve standards of animal care and humane treatment during animal experimentation. But within the academic game of science it is all too easy for the researcher to lose himself in an irrelevant problem, in an intellectual mind-game that may give him the prestige of widespread scientific publication. And he may forget how many animals died for him on his ego trip. A man of science must also be a man of conscience and integrity, constantly assessing the purpose and ethics of his work, whether it involves animals or human subjects.

The day might come when people (or "humanoids") will have electrodes in their brains to control their behavior. Today we use drugs, yesterday we used alcohol. If our brains cannot adapt to the stresses of modern life, our technology can help us. But have we the right, as depicted in the movie *Clockwork Orange,* to control someone else's brain and behavior? The critical point comes with the question of responsibility. If others assume the responsibility for my actions (provided I am not completely deranged), they are controlling me; Thomas Szasz has written at length about this important political aspect of psychiatry. If, however, I abdicate responsibility (or response-ability) for my own behavior, which is the usual problem in most human behavior disorders, then someone must take control. Such control is essential where the welfare of others (rather than the efficiency of the system) is endangered.

In domesticating animals, we have genetically altered their temperaments and brains to adapt them to our way of life. This is true of cattle and pigs, which are more docile than their wild counterparts. It is also true of the dog, something I discussed in detail in my book *Understanding Your Dog*. But what of the cat? From the first chapter it has been clear that man has had little effect on the behavior and, therefore, the brain of the domesticated cat; it is virtually the same as its wild ancestors.

The cat is a night hunter, and although it cannot see in total darkness, its sense of vision is extremely acute in twilight. Most animals that hunt or browse at night—rabbits, deer, foxes, dogs, and cats—have a reflective layer called the *tapetum* at the back of each eye. This structure increases the amount of light passing through the retina and enables the animal to see well when the light intensity is low. Nocturnal animals are, however, insensitive to infrared light, and many naturalists (and hunters, unfortunately) will use such a light on their spotting scope. If human beings had a tapetum, there would be no need for such equipment to enable us to see better in the dark.

One of the reasons why the Egyptians regarded the cat as sacred was because its eyes would glow at night. They believed that the cat's eyes continued to reflect the sun while it was hidden from man; their sun god Ra, who was in the form of a cat, worked against the malevolent powers of darkness.

A cat has a very lively pupil response. At night it dilates to let in as much light as possible, while in the strong sunlight it becomes a narrow slit. In man and dog the pupil is always round, while in the fox and all the cats (except those of the genus *Panthera*) the pupil forms an ellipse during the day. It has been said that the eye tells all (in medieval times it was called the mirror of the soul), and this is certainly true when it comes to a cat's emotions. One can read the pupils of a cat and determine whether it is angry or afraid (see Chapter 5 for further details).

When a cat is concentrating on something, the pupils change shape; this is called accommodation and greatly facilitates accurate distance perception. This rapid pupil reflex, coupled with the location of the eyes in front of the face (rather than to the side, as in a horse or rabbit), enables the cat to calculate the exact distance that it has to leap in order to catch prey. Its eyes are, in fact, better positioned for this task than a dog's.

The retina at the back of the eye contains two kinds of cells, rods and cones. Rods are sensitive to light, cones to color. A cat has more rods than cones, since it must necessarily be very sensitive to light in order to see well enough at night to hunt. Color vision at night would be of little value. The cat's retina has a central area rich in cones, and it is this area that it directs while fixing its gaze on something in the bushes. Because of the structure of its retina, the cat essentially has "movement detectors" that help it locate prey. It may not see a mouse then if it does not move, and this is probably why many animals suddenly "freeze" when they are being chased: The predator might then lose sight of them! Although a mouse might escape if it freezes, the cat's movement detection system is really extremely efficient. With it, a cat does not have to stare at every bush, crevice, or whatever to look for prey. Not taking in any details about the static world, the cat can quickly scan a backyard in a single sweep with its eyes which are "tuned" to detect movement. All other information is irrelevant and is filtered out.

Cats have been trained to select food in darkness from behind one of two panels—one unlit, one dimly illuminated—the illuminated panel having the reward behind it. The cats will make the discrimination between the lit and unlit panels at a level of illumination only one-sixth of that required for man. To the human eye, neither panel appeared illuminated!

Although a cat's eye is infinitely more sensitive than man's, its acuity is about ten times less. If the cat's eye had more cones, its acuity would improve, but some rods would have to be removed to make room for them, so night vision would then be diminished. Until recently it was thought that cats, like dogs, are color-blind, that they are able to see colors only monochromatically (*i.e.,* varying shades of gray, from black to white). Recent investigations, however, indicate that the cat's retina does possess a few cone cells that are sensitive to blue and green; a third red-sensitive cell type is suspected. Thus cats are not color-blind; they at least have dichromatic vision. Most probably, even if the cat is sensitive to some colors, it does not utilize this information in its everyday life, since it relies mainly on other cues—notably movement and sounds—to locate prey (which are usually not brightly colored and are most often camouflaged).

The cat's eye is protected by a membrane—the *membrana nictitans*—which is normally folded into the inner corner of the eye. This membrane is used to protect the eye from dust and debris while the cat is chasing prey, especially into burrows. It also moves partially over the eye when a cat is sick and also when it is relaxed and being petted (see Chapter 7).

Touch is, perhaps, the sense most immediately associated with the cat. Little is known of the function of the whiskers, or vibrissae, on the face of the cat; they may be sensitive to vibrations, but more likely they help to protect the eyes. Flick a cat's whisker and it will close its eyes. A springing twig or sharp blade of grass would touch the whiskers before catching the eye. The whiskers, hooked up by an incredibly fast reflex arc to the eyclids, could trigger the protective eye blink and save the cornea from damage.

Cats love to be stroked and petted, and this is one of the golden shackles that keeps many a cat at home. Cats will solicit stroking by a human being to the point of becoming a nuisance. It is like an opiate for many of them. Often they will "regress" and behave like kittens, alternately extending each forepaw as though nursing and even drooling and nuzzling into one's armpit or neck. This provides a dramatic first clue to what is going on. Right from birth, the mother grooms the kittens, and this is the first sensory experience they receive from another being. Touch is the primal source of affection. Many researchers have shown that in the absence of touch, a human child, an infant rhesus monkey, or puppy will not thrive. It may even die. A mother who keeps the child in a crib and gives it little or no contact will not have a normal child, no matter how clean and well fed it is. Mammals have hair, not only for warmth and protection but for touching, for each other to groom. Each hair has many nerves around it which convey impulses to the brain. Even man, who is not a "naked ape," has millions of fine body hairs that are supplied with many nerve endings for detecting and appreciating touch. The hair on the human scalp is not just to keep the brain cool under the sun, but is a specific body region for social grooming. A good head rub and tickle puts me into ecstasy, and I often maintain that I will be reincarnated as a cat! Chimpanzees will engage in social grooming in the wild for six hours or more. They are not picking lice off each other; they are enjoying touching and being touched. E. T. Hall in his book *The Hidden Dimension* notes how "tactile" members of some cultures are, such as the Mediterranean European, compared to the "hands off" British and Americans. Such differences may be caused by differences in child-rearing practices.

What happens when a dog, cat, or human infant is petted or cuddled? There is a very clear nervous system response (parasympathetic branch of the autonomic system). The heart rate slows, muscle tone drops and the body relaxes; digestion may be enhanced, as digestive juices and saliva flow and peristalsis or digestion movements of the intestines begin.

With fear, discomfort, or deprivation of attention, the opposite happens. It is no wonder that, a few years ago, René Spitz, University of Colorado, found that orphanage infants literally wasted away if they were not cuddled. It would seem that infant mammals need this kind of stimulation for their bodies to grow and function normally. The mother gives them this stimulation, which is rewarding and which subsequently establishes an emotional bond between parent and infant.

Petting an adult dog or cat has the same effect as on a puppy or kitten; the animal relaxes and the heart rate slows way down. For a kitten, such stimulation is perhaps needed for survival, but for an adult it is purely pleasurable. It also reaffirms friendly social relationships. Friendly adult cats will groom each other, one first soliciting, and the other perhaps later being groomed in turn (Figure 12). Such social grooming has evolved much further in chimps and baboons, where grooming is influenced by age, social rank, and degree of sexual receptivity in the female. Social grooming also occurs at a high frequency just after a skirmish has occurred in the troop; it serves, therefore, to reduce tension. In a similar way, an uptight cat will groom itself briefly (see Chapter 7 for further discussion on displacement grooming).

The sense of balance in the cat is legend. As a tree climber, he must have a fine sense of equilibrium, and for this purpose

Figure 12. Socialized adult cats engage in social grooming, a care-giving behavior common in cats housed together

the cat has an extremely well-developed cerebellum and vestibular (balancing) system in the inner ear. A common congenital disorder in cats is *vestibular-cerebellar agenesis*, an underdevelopment of this balancing organ. It may affect just one side of the body so that the kitten tends to crawl in circles with its head and neck twisted to one side. Some improvement may develop after the eyes open and the animal is able to compensate visually.

Seize your cat by its fore and hind legs and hold it up horizontally with its back three feet off the ground above a pillow. Let it go and note how it always twists and lands on all four feet. (A docile and extremely passive cat may not respond to this test initially and just flop on his back or side onto the pillow!) This righting reflex is a remarkable mechanism and must certainly prevent the cat from sustaining severe injury if it does fall out of a tree. Positioned by this reflex, the extended legs, being very resilient, act as landing pads and reduce the chances of the cat sustaining a severe back or internal injury. One of the more elegantly written and photographically appealing, if lightweight, books on the cat (*The Life, History and Magic of the Cat* by Fernand Méry) observes, "A cat that falls from the sixth storey or higher is pitiably crushed to the earth. It breaks a limb if it falls from the first. But it generally escapes well if it falls from the fourth. From the fourth storey the cat has time to turn itself in space; at the same time this height represents the extreme limit for the elasticity of its muscles and the resistance of its bones." Clearly this author should get some pillows and experiment with his own cat! A cat will right itself if dropped from two to three feet off the ground and certainly has plenty of time to do so should it fall from the first floor of an apartment!

Little is known about the sense of taste and smell in the cat. Possibly because of our own poorly developed sense of smell, we have not had the insight necessary to design meaningful experiments on animals. Recently, however, Dr. Jay Rosenblatt has completed a series of elegant experiments on newborn kittens that show that they have a well-developed sense of smell at birth. This enables them to locate the nest and to select their own particular nipple (see Chapter 6 for further details).

The cat possesses a number of scent glands on various parts of the body (see Chapter 5). With the exception of the anal glands, the odors from these other glands cannot be detected by the human nose. Much of the social life of the cat involves scent marking and rubbing behavior, clearly indicating that the sense of smell plays an important role in the cat's life.

Like the dog, the cat possesses a *vomeronasal* (or Jacobson's) organ. Two ducts that lead to this organ are situated in the hard palate just behind the upper incisor teeth. With certain substances a cat will open its mouth (the *flehmen reaction)* to facilitate access of odors to this special olfactory organ. This is especially common when a cat is smelling the work of another cat or is "turning on" to catnip (see also p. 109). In the rabbit, there is a pumplike muscle that helps draw up chemical substances into the vomeronasal organ. Also, this organ in the rabbit connects up to the *amygdala,* a brain center associated with sexual and aggressive (territorial) reactions. Little is known about the behavioral significance of this well-developed organ in the cat. Would blocking the ducts influence sexual behavior or decrease the frequency of spraying and territorial marking?

Two French researchers, Dr. R. David and Dr. G. Thiéry, stimulated, not this organ but the main smell organ with electrodes, and were able to influence the estrus patterns of female cats. Removal of these olfactory bulbs in kittens interferes with their nursing behavior: they were unable to locate a teat to nurse.

As an intriguing side note, it has been shown in mice that

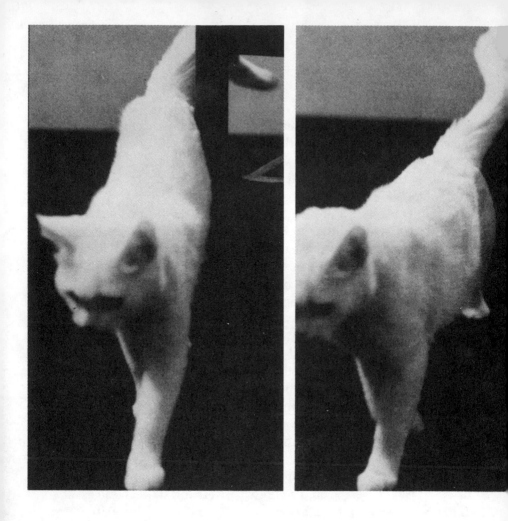

Figure 13. The tail rub against an object occurs during friendly approach and may be a form of scent-marking with the tail gland

Head rubbing marks the person's hand with scent from the temporal gland (See Chapter 5 for further details.)

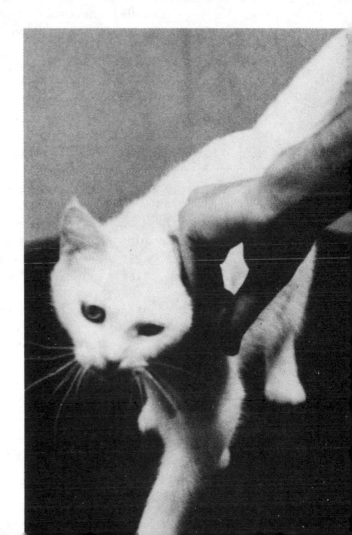

the odor of a strange male will prevent a recently inseminated female from conceiving. Removal of her olfactory bulbs to destroy her sense of smell will prevent this phenomenon from occurring. Place a male mouse in an all-female group and the females will all come into heat three or four days later! Infant female mice also mature more slowly if there is no adult male in their cage. The most remarkable finding, though, is that a male chimpanzee will show *no* interest in an estrus female if his nose is plugged so that he cannot smell her. Even if she is soliciting him sexually, without the vital stimulus of the chemical (or *pheromone*) from her vagina, he will not become sexually aroused.

How important such stimuli are in affecting human behavior remains to be determined. Why do women living together have synchronized menstrual cycles? We should also consider the possible role of odors in a cat colony. Keeping stud males apart from females and kittens may well affect their estrus cycles and sexual development. Much more research is needed in this fascinating area. Meanwhile we continue to use our deodorants and make ourselves anonymous to others in an adaptation to crowding stress. (But the ideal aftershave may be on the way, acting as a sexual attractant, like the urine of a bitch or queen cat in heat, and yet blocking pregnancy like the odor of a strange male mouse. We must find a cure for the common cold first, though, otherwise the whole thing may backfire!)

The last sense that I want to discuss is the sense of hearing. The sensitivity of cats and dogs does not differ very much from that of man at frequencies of up to 500 Hz. At higher frequencies, though, both are vastly superior to man. Some claim that the cat can detect frequencies higher than the dog. Cats can also discriminate one-fifth or one-tenth of a tone that lies within the sound range of maximal sensitivity. The ability to locate sounds is important for a hunter.* Cats can discriminate with 75 percent accuracy between two sound sources separated by an angle of 5 degrees, a performance on the same order as man's. The cat has the advantage of having a mobile external ear, or *pinna,* which it can use to collect sound waves and also scan the environment or direct its attention to a particular source of sound. The direction of the source of sound can also be calculated by the animal sensing differences in the time of arrival and intensity of sound received by the two ears. Certain sounds have a very specific effect, in some cases a consequence of learning. Some of the vocal calls of cats (see Chapter 5), the name its owner gives it, a knock on the door, or sounds of a can being opened act as conditioned stimuli which evoke appropriate learned responses. The best example is high frequency rustling or the sound of scraping. In a kitten this will elicit playful prey-stalking and catching actions. One of my cat's favorite toys is a crumpled piece of cellophane from the outside of a cigarette pack. Such sounds mimic those of small prey which the cat will automatically respond to, even though it may not on first encounter actually kill its prey (see Chapter 5).

In 1932, two French researchers, Dr. M. Bachrach and Dr. G. Morin, reported an intriguing finding. They claimed that the sharp sound *mi* of the fourth octave could act as a powerful genital excitant in cats. The same sound served to establish a conditioned reflex for defecation before puberty. Then, at puberty, it lost its value as a conditioned stimulus for defecation and became absolute for sexual activity. I have not been able to trace any follow-up studies to verify these claims. It may support the notion that the caterwauling of tomcats

---

* Although, interestingly, a number of animals that are preyed upon, especially insects, emit sounds with a ventriloqual quality so that it is extremely difficult for a predator to fix their exact location.

while competing for and courting a queen may excite the tomcats and make the queen more receptive. The role of sounds in producing hormonal changes in mammals awaits further study. The late Dr. Daniel Lehrman of Rutgers University showed that the cooing noises of a male ringdove have a direct effect on the reproductive cycle of the female, accelerating ovary and oviduct development. Perhaps "cat Muzac" in the cattery may liven up those irregular or lazy breeders!

Two other senses—the senses of time and direction—acting together enable the cat to do remarkable things, things hitherto considered extrasensory or psychic. There are some things that defy any rational explanation, though . . . "There are more things in heaven and earth, Horatio, than are dreamt of in your philosophy. . . ."

4

Extra Senses and Super-Cats

SOME FELINE FEATS, when no logical explanation can be formulated, push the rational mind to its limits. Where scientific knowledge or technology to explore these phenomena are lacking, the usual reaction is to dismiss "psychic" phenomena as pure chance or figments of a sensationalist's imagination. The door to further inquiry slams shut and, regrettably, our mechanistic and Cyclopean approach has prevented exploration into the fascinating fringe areas between science and metaphysics. It is heresy for a scientist to venture into metaphysics. A more open-minded approach in the USSR has led to many valuable discoveries and to the establishment of psychical research as a scientific discipline valid in its own right. Interestingly, a number of physicists in the United States (as well as men like former astronaut Edgar D. Mitchell) are now embarking on such exploration, perhaps because modern physics ("meta-physics") has shown that many phenomena defy the usual cause-effect relationship and that unpredictability and variability are perhaps more "natural" than was previously thought. Newtonian physics and Aristotelian logic maintained that all phenomena have a clear cause-effect relationship and a high degree of consistency and predictability. Rigidly adhering to such concepts closed our minds to further discovery.

Another theoretical development of modern physics is field theory, which has great relevance to the interpretation of psychic phenomena. An object or person gives off a certain quantum of energy, a "force field" if you wish, which can be detected by sensitive people. (What senses they use remain to be identified.) An inanimate object can "absorb" some of this energy from a person, and so it is possible for a medium to tell much about a person from his watch or brooch, without ever having met him. Our intellectual insecurity makes us reject such remarkable feats. But it is encouraging that some objective scientific investigation is now under way in this country, especially in view of the widespread negative attitude of scientists and the skepticism caused by those people who claim to have "psychic powers" but instead use trickery to con the public for their own financial and egocentric gain.

In 1950 Dr. J. B. Rhine at his laboratory of parapsychology at Duke University investigated a number of "psychic" phenomena in animals. Four major categories of unusual behavior were identified in the cat: (1) Showing some foreknowledge of a danger threatening it and/or its master. (2) Foretelling its owner's unexpected return home. (3) Finding its way home after being lost several miles from home. (4) "Psi-trailing" to locate its owner in a place where the cat has never been before (those "incredible journeys").

The first two categories involve what might be termed

clairvoyance. But many alleged causes can be explained otherwise. A cat may perceive slight tremors heralding an earthquake or may detect the faint odor of a fire in the house or apartment. Unaware of such low-level stimuli but noting the often bizarre behavior of a disturbed cat that calls to be let out or jumps and claws frantically at the door or windows, the owner may then be alerted to the danger. He may let the cat out and follow it to see what it wanted outside, only to turn around and watch the house collapse or go up in flames behind him. Putting two and two together, the owner concludes that the cat had some forewarning and was attempting to communicate it to him. But, in reality, the cat was simply saving its own skin. More than one cat has awakened its sleeping owners and alerted them to a fire; again one must be cautious and not jump to the anthropocentric conclusion that the cat was intentionally "saving" the household from impending disaster.

As for forecasting the owner's arrival, cats will often go and wait in a favorite spot right on schedule just before its master comes home from work. The cat that suddenly jumps onto the windowsill and prepares to greet its master a minute or so before he arrives unexpectedly might make its mistress believe it has ESP. Very often in such cases the cat hears and recognizes the car or footsteps of its master long before its mistress hears anything, and there is nothing remarkable about this. What is remarkable, though, is the incredible time sense many cats possess. The cat clearly knows what time its master comes home. One of my own cats, Igor, a Siamese, soon learned when I was programmed to get up, and he always woke me with his cold nose on mine two or three minutes before the alarm rang at eight A.M. This was very annoying on weekends, but he did adjust to daylight saving time after three or four weeks when I had to set the clock ahead an hour!

This accurate sense of time is crucially important in nature. A wildcat knows when to go hunting and what time a rival or larger predator might be out and must be avoided. It will synchronize its own daily habits to those of other animals around it, and similarly the domestic cat will adjust its natural rhythms to the household's (see also Chapter 5 for further information on space-time relationships in the cat).

It has been shown in birds that this time sense enables them to use the sun in order to navigate and to find their way home. A cat lost on a camping trip several miles from home finds its way back after a few days. This might seem to be a psychic feat, but it can also be explained on the basis of the cat's exquisite sense of time. Like a homing pigeon, the cat has a physiological internal "clock" which is set to local time (see Figure 14). This internal clock will not correspond to the sun's position in a place, say, one hundred miles from home. A computation of the time difference will give the animal the necessary directional cue toward home. In other words, if it orients itself in the right direction to correct the difference between its internal (home base) time and the actual time where it is at the moment, it will be able to find its way home. Pigeons released to fly home make this calculation immediately and usually set off in a straight line from the point of release *exactly* in line with their home. With their eyes covered with semiopaque lenses, they can still read where the sun is and use it as a compass: Such blindfolded birds will get home without using any landmark cues (since they can't see them). Their ability to use the time clock sun-compass is so accurate that they know when they are right over their roost and will land a few yards away from it!

Dr. Presch and Dr. Lindenbaum in Germany conducted the only experiment I am aware of exploring homing in cats. They collected several house cats and took them varying distances

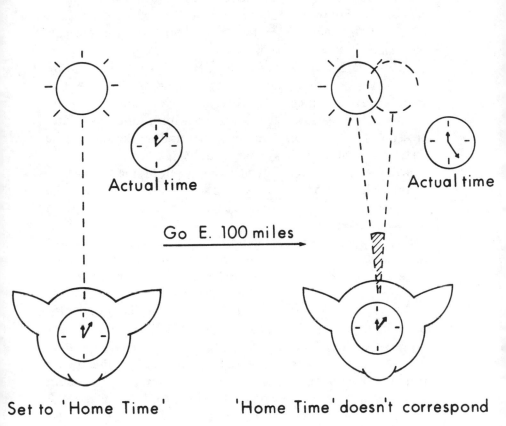

Actual time

Go E. 100 miles

Actual time

Set to 'Home Time'

'Home Time' doesn't correspond

Figure 14. Representation of factors operating in the cat's ability to navigate using the sun as a compass

from their homes. Each cat was placed in the center of a maze that had twenty-four exits arranged in a circle. The cats came out of the exit facing the direction of their homes! This remarkable homing ability tended to drop off with distance greater than twelve kilometers from home, and mature cats performed better than young ones.

In France, a family moved from Buxières-les-Mines to St. Geneviève-des-Bois, a distance of one hundred and sixty-five miles. They took their cats, Mastic and Pinceau, with them. Mastic didn't like the new place, and within nine days, after crossing several rivers somehow, including the Loire, he amazed neighbors by reappearing at his old home.

Monmousse was a pet cat who was lost in Maine-et-Loire in France while the family was on holiday. Ten months later he had made his way home to Doubs, a distance of four hundred and sixty-five miles!

Some people claim that their cat has ESP because it seems to know when they are depressed, or are going out shopping, or leaving the house for the weekend. Again this is a misinterpretation. The cat is an acute observer of human behavior and knows its owner's routine to a tee. Any change in his behavior or routine will be noticed; many cats, of course, show no response, but others, perhaps the more dependent, affectionate, or demonstrative ones, will call, follow the owner from room to room, keep insisting on lying on his lap, attempt to nurse, or even spray or defecate on the rug! (See Chapter 7 for further descriptions of such attention-seeking devices and emotional disorders.)

The most intriguing and inexplicable cases are those of the "psi-trailing" category. Many of these were found by J. B. Rhine to be difficult to verify. The cat had to have a distinguishing feature or collar for exact identification. Someone would claim that their cat had "psi-trailed" them, arriving at their new home, where the cat had never been before, some time after they had left it with relatives or friends in their old neighborhood. Often there was insufficient evidence to support their claims. A marmalade cat, bedraggled and thin, might enter their new house, look like just the cat they had left behind, respond to the name they gave their own cat (a name is often just a call to a cat—often meaning "dinner's ready"). It might behave similarly—playing with a familiar toy, a drape tassel, or wall hanging—and even sleep in the same place "as before" (a comfortable old armchair that any cat would like!).

Often, in such cases, the distance covered was too small to be regarded as psi-trailing, for which a minimum distance of thirty miles was set. Sometimes the distance was too great for the cat to have covered in the time of separation. It really is easy to believe your cat has found you in this way. I was "taken in" once by an emaciated Siamese who found his way to our new home after getting lost six miles away while we were house moving. How wrong I was. This cat was a stray and our own male Siamese turned up a couple of weeks later wandering around its old neighborhood, which we had searched thoroughly for several days!

The verified cases of psi-trailing are, however, quite remarkable. Smoky, a Persian cat with a distinctive tuft of red hairs under his chin, got lost some eighteen miles away from its home in Oklahoma during a roadside stop while the family was moving to Tennessee. Two weeks later, neighbors saw him prowling around the old Oklahoma house for several days. A year later, Smoky appeared at the new home in Tennessee, having covered some three hundred miles.

Sugar, another Persian, would not get into the car that was taking the family from California to Oklahoma, some fifteen hundred miles away. Sugar was given to a neighbor, but after a couple of weeks he disappeared. Fourteen months later

Sugar amazed his household by appearing on their doorstep in Oklahoma! He had the same distinctive callus on the hip and looked otherwise just like the cat they had left behind them.

One of the best-authenticated cases of psi-trailing was of a cat that belonged to a veterinarian in New York. He left the cat in his home area when he moved to take a post in California. Many months later, a cat looking just like his calmly walked into the house and jumped onto its favorite armchair. Not believing his eyes, he felt for the telltale bone growth on the fourth vertebra on his cat's tail, which was the result of an earlier bite injury. And there it was.

Two workers from Rhine's laboratory, Dr. K. Otis and Dr. E. B. Foster, conducted a test for ESP in cats, a test that is often used on human subjects. Food was presented randomly under one of two inverted cups and the cats showed a significant ability to correctly guess where the food was. Their responses should have been 50–50, but, in fact, they responded well above the chance level, indicating that "something" at a higher level of psychic functioning was operating. The experimenters carefully controlled for odor cues, and, of course, the cats did not see under which cup the food was placed. Such laboratory studies are extremely limited and it would be better if more release and homing studies and psi-trailing experiments could be conducted. Unfortunately, many cats in such studies would die from natural hazards during the course of their travels, and the value of such work would have to be weighed carefully against the possibility of inhumane treatment.

These and other phenomena await further investigation by disciplined, objective, and unbiased minds. There are so many vague anecdotes, so few verified cases in both man and animal and so much hocus-pocus as to make the task seem virtually impossible. But the authenticated cases should keep all our minds open to such possibilities and encourage those with the necessary skills and patience to continue scientific investigations. Much remains to be studied, understood, and explained. Why do cats invariably lie on the book that one is reading and, right now, on my notepad as I write this chapter? Get away, Sam! Does Sam want my attention or is he sensing and nosing into my energy field, which is focused totally on this writing task in front of me? Stephen Gaskin in his book *Monday Night Class* noted that a cat will line itself up so as to lie in the direction in which the energy is flowing between two people, where one is giving and the other is more passive and receiving. Is the cat sensitive to such psychic energy fields and directions of energy flow? Is this why a cat lies on your book and is angry if you stroke him the wrong way? Is this why my cats Rocky and Sam always walk into the center of the circle when I have one of my student seminars at home? Is this why a cat will often walk toward someone who is afraid of cats, who has ailurophobia, who is uptight and giving off a lot of energy, a force field, in fact? Being sensitive to energy fields would also account for the cat's "psi-trailing" ability.

5

Social Life
and "Felinese"
Communication

THE CAT IS BASICALLY a solitary species, lacking the degree of sociability and dependency characteristic of the domestic dog and social hunters like the wolf. Domestication and socialization (emotional attachment to the owner) in no way limits the cat's capacity to become feral, or wild. In contrast to many breeds of dog, the structure and behavior of the cat has not been domestically changed by selective breeding, so that almost any cat is capable of fending for itself. In many rural and urban areas the independence of the cat and its drive to roam and hunt make it a serious ecological and public health hazard (see Chapter 8).

Collect ten cats that have never met before and place them in a room; each will invariably stay in one place and there is virtually no interaction; is the experiment a failure since we saw no interaction? No, this, in fact, epitomizes one aspect of feline behavior, in which avoidance of each other rather than close social interaction (except with potential mate or with young) is typical for the species. Place one strange cat in the room of a resident cat, and it may be briefly investigated and then avoided or threatened by the resident. Attacks are rare; the resident may spray, or sniff the ground, or groom itself (an embarrassed displacement act) and then retreat. Interactions of any duration in adult cats are usually limited to sexual encounters and male-male rivalry fights.

Feral cats (domestic cats gone wild) live a relatively solitary life, although their hunting ranges often overlap where they use the same paths or runways. Professor Paul Leyhausen of the Max Planck Institut in Wuppertal, West Germany, has studied cats for many years, and here I will outline some of his findings and also critically review some of his conclusions. One of his studies involved free-roaming cats in rural Wales, and in the cities of Paris, Bonn, Zurich, and Hamburg. He found that cats have a first base "home" territory and also a home range consisting of places for resting, watching, sunbathing, and so on, which are connected by a network of paths and which are visited regularly. In addition, there is an elaborate system of paths that lead to places of congregation, of courting, and of hunting. A high-ranking cat in the area may visit the home territory of an inferior, without violence, but usually such territories are respected.

If two cats happen to meet at the intersection of two pathways, the dominant cat may take precedence; conflicts are avoided by one or both cats sitting and waiting until the inferior backs off or the dominant one, or first comer, takes the initiative. Cats, therefore, regulate their traffic on these pathways by visual contact. Chance face-to-face encounters lead to fighting and chasing, and individuals may then, as a consequence, develop a dominance relationship. Females are apparently less tolerant toward each other than males.

A neighborhood "community" of free-roaming cats does have an order of dominance, but the kind of ranking order produced does not develop into the rigid social hierarchy or peck order that one sees in dogs. For example, if the inferior cat has already entered a communally used passage before the superior cat arrives on the scene, the latter will sit and wait until the way is clear. If it does not, its superiority may be successfully challenged. Dominance in the cat, therefore, also depends on *time and place,* and for this phenomenon of a locality-priority dependent hierarchy, the term "relative dominance" has been coined. Whereas in a group of cats a male may be the overlord (*i.e., absolute dominance*), in particular contexts or at certain times and places another may be dominant over it (*i.e., relative dominance*). The same phenomena have been described in the red fox, the most catlike and solitary of the dog family, in my book *The Behavior of Wolves, Dogs and Related Canids.*

When an owner of a tomcat moves to a new area, he can always expect his cat to come home during the first few weeks all bloodied up from fighting. A newly introduced male cat literally has to fight its way into the group, and may be incited by neighborhood males to come out of its territory to fight (and so gain admission to the "brotherhood"!). For this reason it is often a kindness to castrate males. Their male hormones turn them on to go out and fight and they often get severely injured, as well as becoming a nuisance spraying in the house when rival males come into their territory. Castration removes the desire to go out and fight in many cats, provided it is done early enough in life.

Gatherings of cats, which have nothing to do with mating, often occur at night. They are purely social. A similar coming together has been described in other solitary hunters such as the red fox. The reason for these gatherings is unknown: Perhaps it serves as a kind of population control feedback mechanism. On the other hand, it could be simply a social mixer on neutral territory where a temporary "truce" is declared and respected. Male and female cats will congregate at a meeting place not far from their home range where they sit quite close, even engaging in mutual grooming and licking. Occasional hostility may be seen, such as hissing and ear flattening, but these gatherings are generally peaceful and, interestingly, occur *outside* the mating season. Around midnight the meeting may quietly disperse and each cat will return to its sleeping quarters. At other times and places, these same cats would chase and fight each other. Such meetings do tend to be more frequent and longer, though, as the breeding season comes closer.

Defense of home and home area is intensified in males during the breeding season, although they are more tolerant to trespassers than are females. The latter are extremely aggressive when they are raising a litter.

Although the territorial ranking order described above is relative (and does not deprive the weak of all rights), the rank order of the neighborhood tomcat "brotherhood" is absolute and operates wherever and whenever two members meet. Interestingly, females, both caged and free-roaming, may show a preference for a particular male and in such cases the dominant male does not interfere.

It is unfortunate that there are no further studies on the behavior of free-roaming cats, but studies of social organization in captive colonies do give us further insights into the fascinating social life of the cat. In food competition tests, a clear linear dominance hierarchy, regardless of size and stable over time, is usually evident. There is invariably no clear relationship, however, between dominance and aggression. Cats most aggressive over food are not necessarily the most socially dominant. Sometimes a cat that lost at the food bowl would turn around and swipe at another cat nearby. This is called redirected aggression, the same phenomenon as the executive coming home and taking it out on his wife after the boss has put him down! Besides the clear evidence we've seen for an absolute rank order (dominance hierarchy) at the food bowl, dominance may also be seen at certain other places, such as a preferred resting place. An inferior cat would often leave a favored spot if the dominant cat approached it, but if it did not, the inferior cat would be ignored.

There may also be a prerogative as to the use of space at particular times of day. Some cats use the floor for play and running in the morning and at such times will be superior to others who have "their time" in the evening; again this is independent of their absolute ranking.

Professor Leyhausen also showed an important relationship between the balance of absolute and relative dominance and population density. The more crowded the cage, the less relative dominance is seen, and eventually a despot emerges and also social outcasts, or pariahs, which are victimized by the others.

Clearly, there are severe limitations in studying the domesticated cat in the colony situation since it is basically a solitary species. Even so, a number of important questions can be asked, notably what is the capacity, or behavioral flexibility, of a "solitary" species adapted to one set of ecological variables to adapt to a very different set of conditions? How far can the limits of sociability be pushed in a "solitary" species? A few years ago I was in charge of a research colony of cats and kittens that were needed for research. None were being born and yet the setup looked ideal. They had breeding pairs of cats—one male and one female per cage. Perhaps cats don't like arranged marriages like this, or perhaps they need some competitive stimulation by being together and vying for mates. So I had a large cat room built with trees and resting shelves, and a few weeks later the lab had more kittens than it knew what to do with. One male emerged above all the others, and he alone bred some dozen or more females, or "queens." Why had he never bred when he was alone in a cage with one queen? Social stimulation must clearly play an important role in the sex life of the cat.

Marking Behavior

Cats of either sex, but particularly males, will spray their urine against conspicuous objects—shrubs, posts, and stones. If this were territorial marking to repel other cats, why then should another cat slowly investigate the mark and quietly walk away and show no apparent concern? This marking behavior may not have an intimidating function at all but rather a social function, like leaving a calling card; the same hypothesis has been proposed for the dog in my book *Understanding Your Dog*. It may also serve to space cats out temporally (in time) so as to avoid sudden encounters, and also inform who is ahead and how recently the marker passed by. An animal marking the path that it is using will inform others who may wish to avoid meeting him. This is called *temporal spacing* and was first described in the hippopotamus. These animals use narrow paths that are worn deep by many years of usage. The hippo flails his tail and at the same time shoots out a spray of urine and feces, and like an egg hitting a fan its mark is spread very efficiently. Another hippo coming up behind a short time later will sniff the mark and will wait until he "thinks" the path is clear or will return to the water if contact is to be avoided.

Marking, which consists of backing up, positioning,

trembling of the vertical tail and then spraying, develops in the cat around puberty. The urine passed contains a viscous fatty material that may be selectively voided as a "scent" when marking. Marking increases in males when stimulated by the presence of a female in heat, and is often eliminated by early castration. (The characteristic trembling may persist after castration, though.)

A cat investigating another's mark usually opens its mouth and closes its eyes while sniffing. This is the flehmen reaction, described in Chapter 3, that may facilitate access of the odor to the vomeronasal (Jacobson's) organ.

We have all seen how a cat will rub its head against a chair or along one's leg. This is another long-overlooked aspect of social behavior which Dr. Geoffrey Prescott at Cambridge University, England, has studied in detail. He finds that cats possess scent glands diffusely along the tail *(caudal gland),* and abundantly on each side of the forehead *(temporal gland),* and also on the lips *(perioral gland)* and chin region. Inanimate objects will be marked at certain places and in certain contexts with caudal and perioral glands. Temporal gland marking is associated with friendly head rubbing: Cats that know each other mark each other with their own scent. In the same way, the cat marks its owner!

Clawing (of furniture, etc.) in the housecat may be an exaggerated or *in vacuo* element of territorial marking rather than claw sharpening, *per se,* since this behavior commonly occurs after spraying in many wild Felids. A leopard will back up to a tree and spray and then stand up on its hind legs and rake the tree with its front claws, thus leaving an impressive visual sign of its size, in addition to the olfactory signal.

More recent studies on marking behavior by Professor Leyhausen and co-workers tend, however, to disprove his earlier theory that a cat may be able to tell the freshness of a

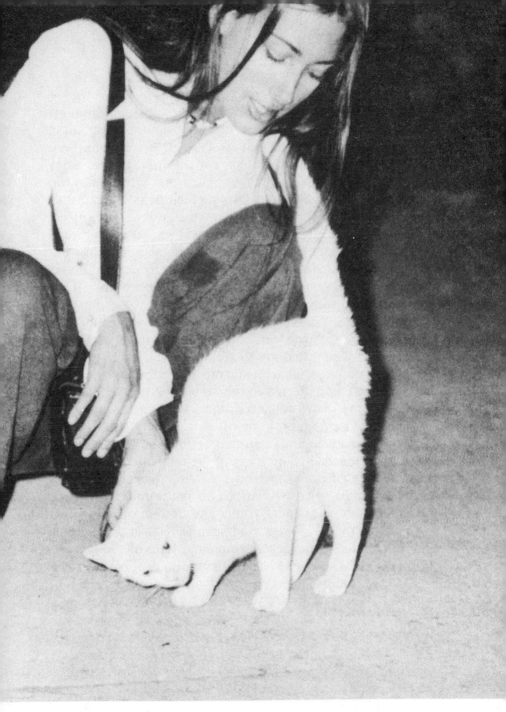

Figure 15. Complex greeting behavior of a night-prowling cat includes friendly vertical tail, posture, tail and head rubbing and bowing, which often follows head rubbing and may terminate in the cat rolling on the ground

mark and so avoid contact with another cat using the same runway. It was found in laboratory tests that cats respond in the same manner to urine that is one or eight hours old. Tests were not run in the field, though, and his original theory may still hold true. Interestingly, they noted that some males will mark with their anal glands, rubbing their behinds against an appropriate object instead of spraying. Also, a cat will not spray over a spot already spray-marked by another (whereas a dog invariably marks the spot where another dog has urinated). Where one cat has rubbed its lips or perioral gland, though, others will mark over with their lips. They experimented with the vomeronasal gland, blocking both ducts and then observing whether the flehmen reaction that occurred after a male cat sniffed strange urine would be eliminated. Their findings were inconclusive. Some cats showed a decrease in flehmen, others an increase, while a number were not affected at all. It is to be hoped that with some of the new advances that have been made in biochemical techniques, some of the scent substances of the cat will be analyzed and identified. In my laboratory we have found that the anal gland scent of the red fox contains more than a dozen different substances. A whole "vocabulary" may be in operation, where variations in concentration of one or more of these substances could give information to other animals as to age, sex, sexual identity (estrus), individual identity, status or rank, and emotional state of the marker; decomposition of some components would also show how recently the animals marked.

"Felinese"

Various body postures and facial expressions are manifest in certain social contexts that serve to communicate mood and intention. A display or body posture signaling one or more emotions is a composite of different units or actions (*e.g.,* tail and ear positions and movement, angle of body, crouch, forward lean, back arch, etc.). Each of these units varies in intensity—amplitude and frequency—so that *successive* shifts in intensity provide information as to the degree of arousal. For example, a cat may hiss threateningly but, if pressed, will growl and swipe with a paw. This increasing intensity of the threat (growling) display communicates a greater readiness or probability to actually attack. The component units of display associated with fear (such as pupil dilation) and aggression (growling) occur not only separately, as when the cat is afraid or aggressive, but also *simultaneously.* When they are combined or superimposed in this way, we know that the cat is ambivalent; fear and aggression signal defensive threat. Thus, with this capacity to successively shift the intensity of signals and to make simultaneous combinations, the cat has a rich and variable communication repertoire.

Since many of the displays are basically composed of simultaneous combinations of increasing and decreasing degrees of fear and aggression, Professor Leyhausen concludes that the cat lacks any display of submission in its repertoire. A reevaluation of the displays does not support this contention (see Figure 16). Three basic categories are evident, namely, offensive threat, defensive threat, and a passive crouched posture. (From the latter crouched posture the cat may roll over and claw to defend itself.) The offensive threat display is simply a direct stare with body poised in intention to rush and strike. In defensive threat, the effectiveness of the back-arch display is enhanced by the animal presenting itself sideways to its adversary. Simultaneous combinations lead to composite postures and compromise movements, as when the anterior region is more on the defensive than the hind region of the body. A cat will then "crab walk," leading with its hind

91

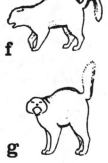

Figure 16. Body postures during different motivational states (modified after Leyhausen, 1973). (a–c) increasing offensive display; (a–e) increasing passive submission. Cat may roll over in (e) into defensive posture. (a–g) increasing defensive threat display

legs! (The hind end of the cat is literally less afraid than the front end!)

The passive crouched posture closely resembles the passive submissive, or surrender, posture of the red fox and may be correctly regarded as a passive submissive display in the cat. It may effectively "cut off" an attack and appease an aggressor.

The appeasement display of dog and wolf also includes *rolling* over onto one side (and submissive urination). Such behavior in the cat is not incorporated into its submissive display but does occur during courtship ("rolling of the queen") and during play as a play-soliciting, or invitational, gesture, as in the red fox (see Figure 17), although cats never urinate submissively like dogs.

The active submission "greeting" display of wolves and dogs contains a number of action patterns "derived" from infancy, such as whining, pawing, head pushing, and licking like a puppy approaching its mother to nurse. Similarly, in the cat, active submissive greeting includes a vertical tail posture, which is seen earlier in life when a kitten approaches or follows its mother (see Figure 18). The adult cat runs for its owner when called, with its tail stuck high in the air. The tail position may be an infantile posture "derived" from the mother licking the anogenital region of the kitten to help it evacuate and also to clean it. This has been interpreted as a sexually derived social presentation in greeting by other authorities, and it does look as though the cat is positioning itself sexually (see Figure 19). When one follows the development of this display through, it becomes quite clear that the adult cat behaving this way, male or female, is acting like a friendly infant. Such behavior between cats is often followed by one sniffing and licking the hindquarters of the other, *i.e.,* acting like "mother."

As an interesting side note, the groin presentation, rolling

Figure 17. Rolling display of a leopard in heat and an Abyssinian cat during play

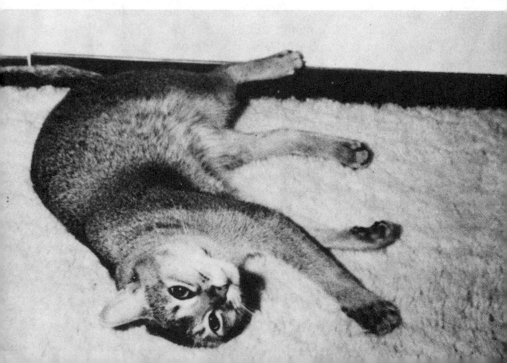

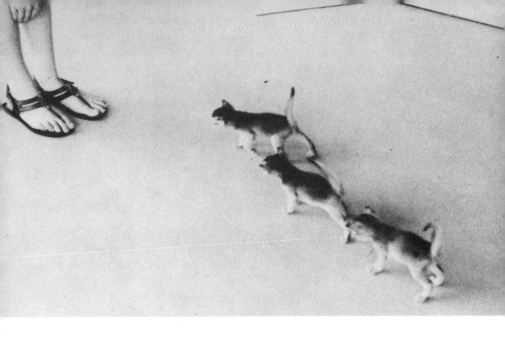

Figure 18. The following response in kittens to a person and to their mother. Note vertical tail display during approach

Figure 19. Anogenital presentation and tail raising in cats soliciting food and in greeting (opposite)

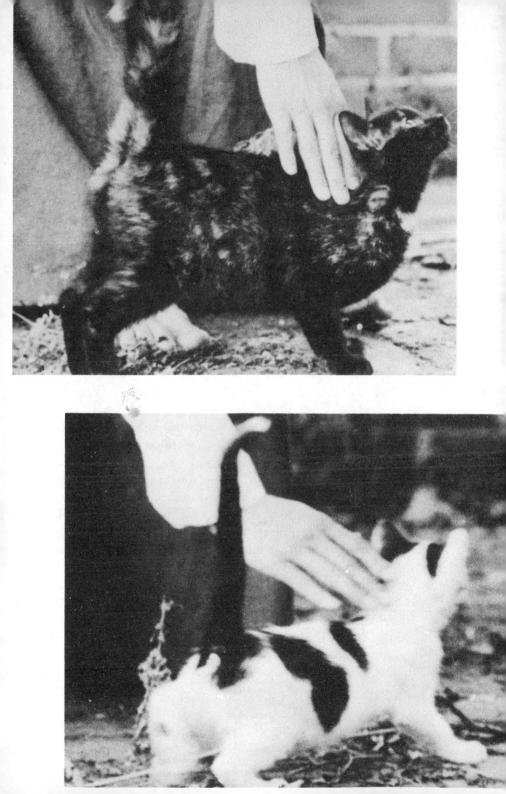

over, and submissive urination in the adult dog is related to the infant pattern of remaining still while the mother cleans the pup. Touch a dog on the groin and it will remain quite still.

Another example of a "derived" behavior (a behavior that shifts into another context) is seen in baboons. A male or female will present itself sexually to a high-ranking male or female and the latter will mount it and show a few pelvic thrusts. This is not sexual behavior or a homosexual perversion. These sex-related acts have evolved to fulfill another function, namely, as signals of submission and dominance. The dominant one mounts, the subordinate presents. Similarly, a male cat will mount, tread, and bite the scruff of a low-ranking male that crouches in passive submission. The dominant male is asserting rank and is not always behaving homosexually (although homosexuality is not uncommon in the cat—see Chapter 7).

When two cats meet, social investigation may take place and the areas of the body they investigate tie in with where some of the scent glands described earlier are located. One cat will take the initiative and sniff the anus (where there are perianal scent glands), or temporal or mouth region, where scent glands are also located. Nose touching and, with more friendly encounters, head rubbing occurs.

Actual fighting among males is normally "ritualized," bites and claw rakes being directed toward the shoulder and neck region, these regions being protected by much thickened skin. This thickened skin is possibly a secondary sexual characteristic (*i.e.*, developed under the influence of sex hormones), and develops even in males that have never fought.

The thick cheeks of the tomcat give him a fuller face, which is all the better to display with. The bigger-looking the face, the more intimidating it would be to a rival. This is why the lynx has its cheek feathers (see Figure 7 in Chapter 2) and the lion a mane. Castrate a young lion and its mane doesn't develop. This incredible display structure is used for frontal threat—the lion roars and his display is enhanced by the great mane. So he always *faces* his adversaries; to display sideways-on would not show off the mane to its fullest. The domestic cat doesn't have a mane, although the thickened cheeks of the tomcat are perhaps a rudiment of it. So the cat, without a superstructure to enhance a frontal threat display, will instead turn sideways and arch its back, fluffing out the hair on its back and tail in order to intimidate a rival. It gives the same illusion, making the cat seem much larger than it really is. With its mane, the lion has no need to arch its back; and, in fact, it does not have such a display in its repertoire. A confident cat will threaten head on, but one on the defensive will turn side-on and give the back-arch display since his head, unlike the lion's, is not impressive enough!

This leads us into an intriguing area of the anatomy of behavior, where certain body marks and structures have some behavioral significance. A black or white tail tip or light and dark rings enhance tail movements and displays, and likewise the ear tufts of a lynx or caracal (see Figure 20), and the white spot on each ear of the tiger enhances ear positions associated with various displays. The color of the coat—stripes, spots, or brindle-brown—help in concealment for hunting purposes. But these are mysterious, too. Are the spots on a cougar kitten (see Figure 21) an ancestral mark that disappears with maturity, or do they serve as a special sign to adult cougars that this is an infant to be cared for and not harmed?

A number of other tail postures are seen in different contexts (see Figure 22). It is obvious that the tail displays of the cat are much more differentiated than was previously believed.

Facial expressions, compared to the dog, are less highly

Figure 20. An abrupt change from relaxation (opposite) to threatening hiss and canine teeth display in a Serval

differentiated in the cat. These expressions associated with offensive and defensive threat are schematized in Figure 9 (note that the pupil is constricted in offensive threat and dilated when the cat is fearful). In addition, other expressions include: the flehmen response; passive submissive looking away with half-closed eyes and flattened ears; the "consummatory face," where eyes are half-closed and membrana nictitans sometimes relaxed, as during petting, social grooming, eating, defecating, and copulating; the wide-eyed, ears-forward play face. As in the dog, a direct stare is also used in the cat to regulate social distance. As one cat walks past another, the latter may pursue it but will stop within a critical distance of three to four feet if the other cat suddenly stops and looks at it. Crouching without staring or looking back is a submissive gesture, and, if given by a female in heat, it may be a signal inviting the male to approach (see later).

Vocalizations

Cats emit a variety of vocal sounds: Sixteen different voice patterns have been distinguished and classified under three main groups: *murmur patterns* in friendly relaxed state, *e.g.*, rhythmic repeated purr while being petted and a single "purr" contact sound; *vowel patterns,* more articulated sounds associated with care-soliciting and goal-frustration (*e.g.*, meow for food); *strained intensity* sounds, in attack, defense, and mating (*e.g.*, hiss and growl-scream). Purring is first associated with nursing, while the distress meow of a kitten can be different for each member of the litter. To what extent the mother uses such cues to identify individuals remains to be tested. Some domestic cats have a growl-bark when alarmed (the bobcat does actually bark like a dog). Tomcats use a

Figure 21. A puma, cougar, or mountain lion cub; note the spots, which disappear with maturity and may be an important social signal of infancy

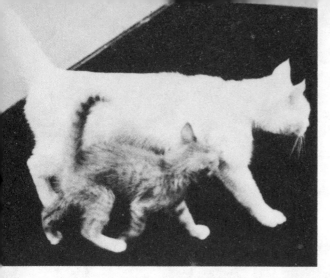

Vertical tail, friendly
approach to mother

Figure 22. TAIL POSTURES IN VARIOUS CONTEXTS

Vertical with piloerection, moderate
intensity threat

Arched tail, high arousal during play

Inverted U tail, especially
when being chased in play

Arched tail with piloerection,
defensive threat

Inverted U tail with piloerection,
intermediate offensive-defensive
threat

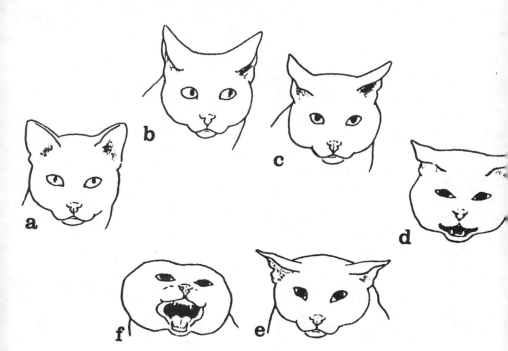

Figure 23. Facial expressions in different motivational contexts (modified after Leyhausen, 1973). Note changes in ear position and pupil dilation. (a) Alert. Offensive threat in (b) with fear increasing in (c). Ambivalent offensive-defensive expression in (d) shifting to increasing defensive threat in (e) and (f)

distinctive coaxing call to lure young males out of their homes to fight. During courtship the female often emits a sharp purr-call that is an acceptance-to-mount signal to which the male appropriately responds. If he attempts to mount in the absence of such a call, he may be rebuffed. Much more work is needed on cat vocalizations, especially those between mother and infant (calling to food, warning growl which sends them to cover) and, as noted earlier, nothing is known of the possible behavioral and hormonal effects on the female of males' "caterwauling."

No one has been able to give me a good explanation of the phenomenon of purring other than to say that a cat does it when it's contented. Could it mean the same thing to cats, and how did it evolve? At the zoo one day I heard two brown bear cubs nursing; they each made a loud purring noise like two motorbikes. I have never heard any member of the dog family making this particular sound. If a kitten first does it while it is nursing, why doesn't it choke? Purring occurs while the kitten is breathing in and out and momentarily stops between swallows. It may be an important signal to the mother facilitating the letdown of milk. Cattle become conditioned to various sounds at milking time that facilitate this milk letdown into the milk cisterns of the udder, and a human mother may feel milk gush from her breasts when her infant cries. As a cat matures, purring becomes a signal of friendly approach and is used to maintain contact. Unlike dogs and wolves, cats have few infantile signals in their repertoire as adults to communicate their friendly intentions to one another. In an adult cat, purring may be analogous to the licking, paw raising, and nose pushing of the adult dog, actions which, in the dog, are first seen during nursing. Purring in cats, then, is a "derived" infantile signal. This notion is supported by the fact that an adult cat will often completely "regress" and not only purr but also salivate, make sucking movements with the mouth and alternately push the front paws as though it were nursing.

Sexual Behavior

Puberty in the female occurs between three and a half and nine months; seven months is the earliest age for puberty in the male. Females born in February can have a heat period in May or June, but if born in April, they may not come into heat until the following year. Free-ranging females may not reach puberty until fifteen to eighteen months. The heat, or estrus, has a three-week periodicity; receptivity lasts from four to six days if the queen is mated and six to ten if she is not mated. Often there is an extended "potential" estrus that can be triggered by the introduction of a male.

The peaks of estrus are mid-January through March and May through June in northern latitudes and in southern latitudes the first seasonal peak is earlier. The long *anestrus* (quiescent phase) between late September and early January can be broken by giving the cats more artificial light. Increasing daily illumination to twelve hours in September can shift the first estrus to November instead of January. Although normal experienced males will copulate any time of the year, there is evidence that males also have a sexual cycle.

The courtship fighting and displays of the males may promote maturation of the female's ovarian follicles or eggs. The exact timing of ovulation is reflexively triggered by intromission when the male enters the female, since the cat reflexively ovulates with vaginal stimulation.* The male has a

* Artificial stimulation with a Q-tip, for example, may effectively terminate repeated heats in pet cats, notably Siamese, and is safer than hormone treatment.

penis covered with small spines, which must cause considerable stimulation (see Figure 24). Unlike the dog, false pregnancy in the cat is rare and occurs only after she has had an infertile mating. Her abdomen will swell; she may seek a place to make into a nest and will occasionally produce milk. Some cats in this condition will adopt a toy or small object and carry it around and treat it like a kitten!

Courtship and copulation is a remarkably synchronized sequence of events (see Table 1). In experienced breeders, though, some of the preliminaries may be omitted, and in naïve males intromission may not occur at first.

Before sexual behavior is initiated, the male will investigate the area and mark it with anal gland and urine spray. Each male has its own particular style of mating and soon learns not to approach head-on but sideways from behind and only when the female shows *lordosis* (lowers her front end and lifts up her hindquarters); otherwise he may be rebuffed. Adjustments between individual males and females are reciprocal; the behavior of the male elicits sexual posturing in the female, and she, in turn, arouses the male to further sexual activity. Place a male in a strange place or with a strange female, and there is often some delay until mating synchrony is established. It is a good rule, then, to take the queen to the stud and allow him to breed her in his own familiar territory.

Experienced pairs may mate ten times in an hour. Male cats mated to "exhaustion" show recovery when placed with a fresh female, while female cats become more willing to mate with experience. Some queens will accept only one particular male of their preference, while others will mate in succession with several males in a group.

Catnip (containing the chemical cis-trans-nepetalactone) has been thought to be a feline aphrodisiac. Catnip does release body rolling and face-rubbing, which usually occur

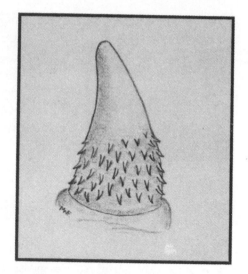

Figure 24. The penis of a mature cat is covered in small spines which must cause intense vaginal stimulation in the female and therefore may facilitate ovulation

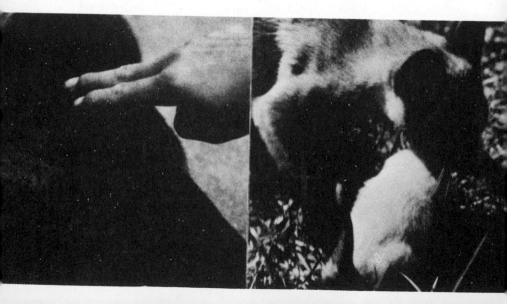

Figure 25. A female Siamese rolls in courtship display to a naïve if not nonplussed male (above). When touched at the base of the tail, she "presents" and treads with her hind feet (below left), a clear sign of heat. She retrieves her one kitten by seizing it by the scruff (below right); the kitten remains immobilized when this region of the body is held

Table 1. *Courtship, Copulation, and Post-Copulation Interactions* *

		Male Cat	Female Cat
Courtship Phase[†]		calls, roams, and sprays	calls, roams, and sprays
		⟷	
		follows female trail	
		⟷	
		sniffs genitalia of female	meets male **
		⟷	⟷
		(gives flehmen reaction)	crouches
			⟷
		⟷	rubs nose and mouth
			⟷
		circles female	rolls
		⟷	⟷
		mating call	calls
		⟷	⟷
		runs toward female	treads

| *Copulation Phase* | 1–3 minutes | grips neck of female
mounts with front legs
straddles with hind legs
rubs with forepaws
makes stepping movements
arches back
pelvic thrusts
penis erects
pelvic lunge | crouches **

treads

swings tail to one side
raises hind end
vulva dilated |
| | 5–10 seconds | intromission
ejaculation
penis withdrawn | copulatory cry
pulls forward
turns on male |

| *Post-Copulation Phase* | | licks penis and forepaws

sits near female | licks genitalia
rolls
rubs nose and mouth
licks paws
watches and may paw male |

* Table adapted from data of Dr. Rosenblatt and Dr. Aronson, Rutgers University.
[†] Later sequences of courtship phase may last from 10 seconds to 5 minutes.
** May initially run from or repel male.

when a cat is in heat. But these reactions to catnip occur independent of sex—they occur in castrated cats; also, catnip does not increase sexual activity in cats. One may conclude that catnip releases behavior similar to the estrus display of rolling, but this behavior is not exclusive to estrus, *per se,* and also that catnip is not an aphrodisiac!

Although testosterone, the male sex hormone, is secreted before the fourth month and stimulates development of the penile spines, mating does not usually occur until eight or nine months of age. Castration at four months, just prior to puberty, abolishes all mating behavior, but this can be induced following testosterone treatment. Castration after puberty causes a variable decline in sexual behavior, there being a greater retention of sexual activity in those males that have had prior sexual experience. Castrating an older tomcat may, therefore, not stop him from spraying or wanting to go out and roam or fight.

Unlike pups, kittens show little "sex play"; mounting, with or without scruff biting, is seen rarely during social play. Also, unlike dogs, females in heat rarely show the male mounting pattern to another female or to a passive male. Normal tomcats may occasionally show the female pattern of lordosis when mounted by another male, but as emphasized earlier, this may simply be a submissive posture. Confined males will often display sexual behavior toward other animals or substitute inanimate objects. Often, rather bizarre relationships develop between a cat and dog in a household, each taking turns to be mounted. The patterns of sexual frustration in confined pets will be discussed in more detail in Chapter 7. Females, notably Siamese, often have prolonged heats and show *hyperarousability* (nymphomania). I have had more than one call from distraught but naïve owners who thought their cat was going crazy from some disease, poison, or brain tumor.

113

The behavior of a horny queen can be very disturbing to the uninitiated!

Maternal Behavior and Mother-Infant Interactions

Pregnancy lasts from sixty-three to sixty-five days. Cats do not form pair bonds and the male leaves the female after copulating; it is not uncommon, though, in house cats for males to show some paternalism toward kittens. A few days prior to *parturition* the female seeks a dark, quiet place for the delivery. Parturition, as in all mammals, consists of four phases—namely, contraction, emergence, fetus delivery, and passing of placenta. The interval between delivery of kittens is variable and emotional disturbances (interference, fear, etc.) may prolong the process. Cats dependent on their owners may delay parturition if the owner is not with them, or refuse to use a designated nesting area in preference to an area where they would be closer to their owner. Why should a cat who always sleeps on the bed be banished from her favorite spot when she is about to deliver? The best rule of thumb is to let the cat herself choose where she wants to have the kittens; encourage her subtly with a nest box lined with newspaper. Leave her alone to deliver—just look but don't interfere; otherwise complications may well arise.

Delivery is heralded by the breaking of the fetal sack. An inexperienced cat licks up the fetal fluids indiscriminately from herself, the floor, and from the emerging kitten, but, with experience, attention is focused more directly on the kitten. Licking reflexively stimulates respiration. All the kittens are eventually licked dry, and the mother rests in a recumbent semicircle around them. Any kitten crawling away from her will be touched with a paw or licked in order to orient it

114

toward her side. Within one hour after parturition is over, the kittens are usually nursing. As with most mammals, the cat eats the placentae (which might provide some nutrients and a hormone, *oxytocin*, to potentiate milk letdown) and severs the umbilical cord with the shearlike *carnassial* teeth.

For the first two weeks the mother comes to the kittens at regular intervals and lies down to let them nurse. There is strong evidence that kittens develop preference for a particular teat, which reduces competition and provides optimal stimulation for continued and productive lactation. Sucking becomes restricted to one teat after a few days, but this declines with age. Before this decline, a kitten will reject a strange mother's teat but will accept it when specificity for its own mother's teat begins to decline. No such teat preference has been observed in puppies.

The anal and genital regions of the kittens are licked by the mother to reflexively stimulate urination and defecation. She ingests such materials, and this effectively keeps the nest clean until the kittens are mature enough to leave the nest and eliminate by themselves. She also grooms them, retrieves wanderers with a scruff-hold, and may show brief rudiments of play behavior that become more frequent and elaborate as the kittens mature and become more responsive to her and to each other.

By the middle of the third week, the kittens occasionally leave the nest area and, from this time on, begin to approach and follow the mother and to initiate nursing themselves. From around the fifth week on, maternal behavior declines, the kittens begin to take food from other sources, and the mother leaves them alone more frequently and for longer periods. Some mothers will actively jump out of the way of their boisterous offspring and show obvious annoyance at their rough and playful antics. Other mothers are more permissive and allow the kittens to maul them and will often wrestle and chase them.

In summary, there are three major phases of mother-infant interaction in nursing. In the first phase, the female initiates feeding by going to the kittens in the nest; in the second phase, feeding is initiated by a reciprocal interaction of female and young; and, in the third stage, suckling is initiated mainly by the kittens.

When the kittens are five or six weeks old, feral and farm cats begin to bring dead and later live prey for their offspring, and may also take them out on hunts. None of the cat species carries food in its stomach and regurgitates it for its offspring, while all members of the dog family do so. Weaning is a gradual process, however, and suckling may continue for several months, especially when one kitten is confined with its mother. A generational order in this prolonged suckling was seen in three cats: a grandmother, mother, and daughter each had a litter of kittens. The mother nursed off the grandmother, the daughter off both, and the grandmother off neither!

A cat with young offspring may readily accept strange kittens, but as hers mature she tends to avoid or reject introduced kittens. One female cat showed ambivalent behavior to a strange kitten, her response depending on which end of the kitten she contacted first. She happened to approach it first from the rear, sniffed its anogenital region, and at once started toilet licking; the kitten turned around, and on smelling its face, the female hissed and struck at it with her paws!

Hunting Behavior

One of the most fascinating and best-studied aspects of cat behavior is the development of hunting and prey-killing. A mother cat will bring dead prey and eat it in front of the kittens, and soon they will eat with her. As they mature, she brings live prey. A few years ago the farm cottage in which I lived was soon overrun with field mice. My Siamese cat was a little too zealous about providing live prey for her kittens. Six months later we still had her mice living inside our piano for the winter! Mothers may help their kittens with killing and will retrieve prey if it escapes before they have killed it; later they may take them out on hunts. Clearly, the kittens learn much from the mother by observation and imitation, although the action patterns of prey catching and killing are innate or unlearned. These actions include a stalking run, crouch stalk, pounce, forepaw grab and pin, and a killing bite (without the doglike head shake). The neck-directed prey-killing bite may be an *innate taxis,* a fixed inherited response, visual orientation being guided to the constriction between the head and body of the prey. Movement of prey and rustling sounds are also important visual and auditory releasers and are mimicked by all of us getting a kitten to play with a ball or a string or a wad of crinkly paper.

The neck-bite orientation and strength of the bite does improve with experience. After noting that a cat will move its nose along the body of its prey sometimes before striking, Professor Leyhausen used a series of different "skin sausages" of rats (with tail present or absent; head present, absent, or attached to hind end; or head, body, or both head and body skinned). He concluded from these studies that the orientation of the neck bite is also guided by tactile cues, namely the direction of the lie of the hair (or feathers, if it is a bird). The incredibly accurate and fast neck bite may involve not only visual and tactile cues, but, in addition, possibly to accomplish the complete bite that must pass between the vertebrae to sever the spinal cord, the cat must "feel" with its canine teeth.

Special nerve receptors are abundant around the base of the canine teeth for this purpose, and little time is lost in searching for the right spot to bite since the jaw muscles can contract with remarkable speed.

Proficiency in mouse killing increases as a kitten matures, but after a few months a kitten never exposed to live prey before may never kill. It will stalk and chase and paw the mouse but never execute the killing bite. There may, therefore, be a critical period early in life for the development of prey killing (see Figure 26). The action patterns of stalking and ambush, as well as the chase response to small moving objects, appear in play long before the kitten is old enough to make its kill. Thus, when the mother brings home live prey when the kittens are two and a half to three months old, the neck bite may be absent or only partially executed. Excitement from play with the prey or competition with littermates ultimately breaks the inhibition of the bite and the kitten kills for the first time. In the 1930's Zing-Yang Kuo from Ceylon, now residing in Hong Kong, studied the effects of early experience on the development of prey killing. He found that (1) kittens reared with mothers who killed either rats or mice in their presence killed rodents earlier and more often than (2) kittens not having such exposure; even so, half of the latter group killed a mouse or rat. Kittens of the first group tended to kill the kind of prey they saw their mother kill, and only later did they kill other kinds of prey. Only three out of eighteen kittens raised *with* rats or mice killed prey (if they were raised with a mouse, they would kill only a rat, and vice versa). When exposed to rat-killing adult females, these latter kittens showed no increase in prey killing, whereas the kittens of group two did. Hunger did not affect prey killing. The old story that a hungry cat will catch more rats and mice is not true. A well-fed and healthy cat is likely to catch more. Hunger can motivate killing in an experienced cat, but it is

118

virtually without effect in an inexperienced one. The connection between making a kill and eating it (or realizing that it is food) has to be learned. Cats raised on a vegetarian diet also killed prey (although the dead prey was less often eaten then!).

It is extremely common for a cat to play with a mouse, postponing the killing bite for some time. It may seem that the cat has a cruel streak, putting off the coup de grace until the last moment. The repetition of prey-chasing and catching actions may be very rewarding and pleasurable to the cat, especially one that has been confined and given no access to prey for a while. A high arousal state may be responsible for the continuation of prey-catching "play" in a cat that has just killed prey after a long struggle. The actual leap at the prey is calculated so that the *hind* paws land just beside the prey first, so that the forepaws are free to grab the prey at the moment of landing. Some domestic cats are extremely adept at catching birds, being able to seize the bird with one leap into the air, catching it in one or both forepaws and instantly biting it. Of the wild cats, the serval and caracal are perhaps the most adept bird-catching specialists. One cat from Malaysia, the fishing cat, is extremely skilled at hooking fish with its fore claws. Domestic cats on the west coast of Scotland and in other coastal areas will wade into the shallows and catch fish.

Play Behavior

Play behavior develops in the kitten around the third week of life, various action patterns appearing with increasing age. Face- and body-oriented pawing and occasional biting are first to develop. Later, chasing, stalking, leaping, rolling over, and wrestling with hindfeet kicking and forelimb clasping

Figure 26. Cats not exposed to live prey as kittens will often ignore them. . .

Or engage in play without injuring the mouse at all

The chase (left); leap and catch (below cent...

Figure 27. ACTIONS DURING SOCIAL PLAY IN KITTENS DERIVED FROM PREY-CHASING AND FIGHTING ACTIONS. NOTE VARIOUS TAIL POSITIONS

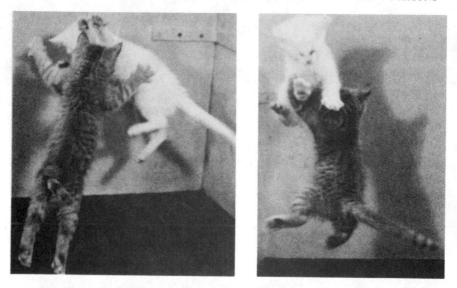

Reversal of roles, the chasee now chases its partner

efensive posture,
"stand-off"

Defensive pawing

Roles are reversed again and the other kitten assumes a defensive
"stand-off" posture

Back arch threat   Defensive pawing

Figure 28. ACTIONS DURING INTENSE SOCIAL PLAY INCLUDE THOSE OF
ACTUAL FIGHTING

Frontal approach and threat by white cat (above) and defensive crouch
by partner (below)

Defensive rolling over

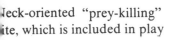

Neck-oriented "prey-killing" bite, which is included in play

Rare sexual mounting during play.

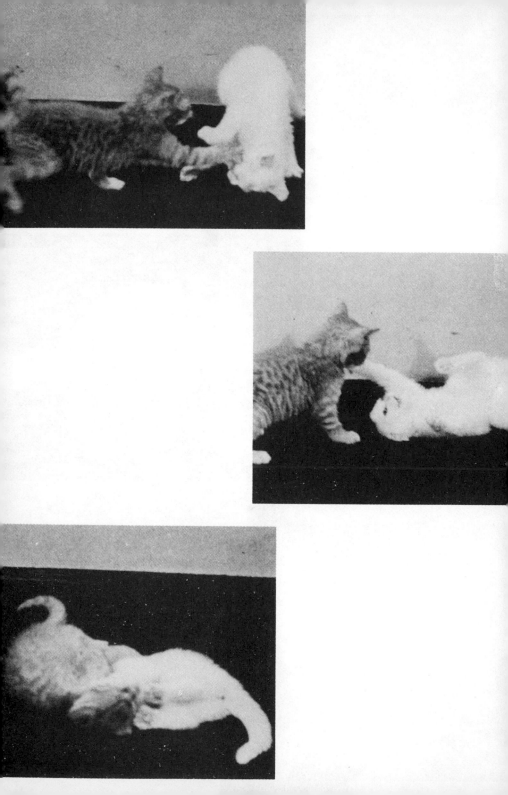

Figure 29. The defensive flip-over occurs during playful fighting. When threatened, the white kitten quickly flips over and rakes its partner with its hind claws (opposite), often grasping its adversary between its forepaws (this page)

Figure 30. ACTIONS OF
SELF-PLAY IN A KITTEN

Tail chasing (this page)

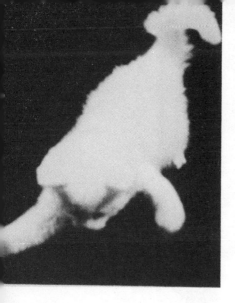

Chasing imaginary prey between paws

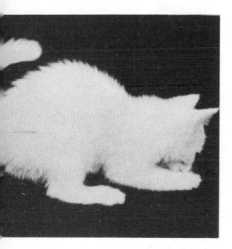

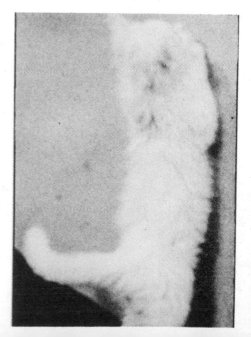

Leaping at wall and catching imaginary fly

Figure 31. The play-soliciting posture of the cat is a rolling onto one side which is similar to the rolling of a cat in heat

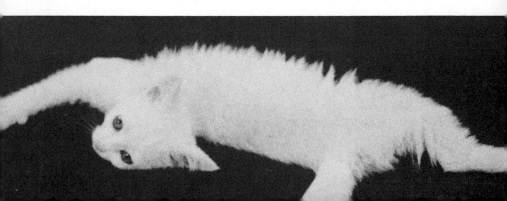

Stalking crouch (above) and stalking run (below) are prey-catching actions which occur frequently during social play

around the neck of the partner develop. Actions associated with fighting, chasing, and prey catching are incorporated into the repertoire of social play (see Figures 27–29). Inanimate object play (with a ball or stuffed mouse) and self-play such as tail chasing are composed essentially of prey chasing and catching actions. An *in vacuo* "hallucinatory" play occurs in at least two forms in the kitten, namely, leaping at the wall and catching nonexistent things and pawing, batting, and chasing along the ground some invisible thing between the forepaws. A phantom mouse perhaps! (See Figure 30). It is unlikely that play serves any function in perfecting hunting skills, but rather it serves to expose the developing organism to the environment. Play with peers leads to social attachments and development of social relationships; play and exploration of inanimate objects can lead to a knowledge of where to find food and what can be eaten (insects, small reptiles, birds, and rodents). Social play may reinforce relationships among adults and between parent and young. The display of rolling over (see Figure 31), like the play bow in the dog, is used to solicit social play.

It has been said that those animals that play and explore a lot in their infancy will be more intelligent than those that have a short period of infancy and play and explore very little. This is quite true, in fact, of all the mammals; the carnivores (including dogs and cats) and primates (man and ape) are the most intelligent. A child, puppy, or kitten deprived of play and the freedom to explore early in life may not only suffer from emotional problems later in life, but may also experience learning difficulties and have a lower I. Q. A number of factors may affect development early in life; some can ruin a potentially good kitten while other treatments can bring out the best in the animal. These aspects of behavior development, relevant not only to raising kittens but also to raising children, are remarkably intriguing.

6

Growing Up

BETWEEN FOUR AND five weeks of age a kitten's brain is almost fully mature. It has the senses of an adult by this age. But its motor development—the fine skills of tree climbing, running away from a dog, and being able to catch prey and fend for itself in the wild—takes much longer to develop. As in a human infant, senses mature before locomotion and refined motor skills. The five-week-old kitten also lacks experience; it will not know that things are dangerous and it has much to learn if it is to survive.

During the first week of life a kitten spends most of its time nursing and in a state of sleep known as activated, or REM, sleep. In the adult this sleep state is associated with dreaming (yes, cats *do* dream). But what does a deaf and blind neonatal kitten have to dream about? Watch it as it lies and quivers and twitches in the nest. During this state of sleep, which may be vital for development, a center in the brain sends impulses to other parts of the brain to stimulate the growth of new connections.

The most well-developed sense in a neonatal kitten is the sense of smell. Dr. Jay Rosenblatt of Rutgers University has shown that a newborn kitten rapidly learns the smell of its own nest. When it is removed from the nest, it will show distress and call for its mother because it is in a strange place that smells different. If a kitten is placed a few feet outside the nest box, it will crawl around and eventually find its way back. Repeat the procedure a few times and it will get back faster, yet its eyes are still closed! Apparently the kitten is able to follow its odor trail back to the nest. Dr. Rosenblatt also showed that a kitten raised on an artificial mother will prefer a teat of a particular taste and texture. Teat preference in kittens raised normally, therefore, may depend on the odor and texture of the mother's nipples, each nipple probably having a slightly different odor and texture!

A four-week-old kitten will show little distress in a strange place if it can see other kittens, in contrast to a younger one whose eyes have not yet opened. Distress in the latter kitten would stop as soon as it is put back (even alone) into its familiar smelling nest box. Perhaps this olfactory attachment to the nest area is important in the wild, for it stops kittens from straying out of the den when the mother is out hunting.

All kittens are appealing, and any would seem to be a potentially good pet. Before choosing a kitten though, it is a good idea to get some information about the temperament of the breed you have in mind. Second, when you go to look at the litter, see if the mother is friendly or fearful. Timidity can be inherited and transmitted to the offspring, possibly appearing at a later age in the kitten some time after you have bought it. Observe how the kittens interact with one another and arrange to see them at feeding time. One could then avoid inadvertently choosing a very dominant and assertive one or a submissive and timid one, neither of which would make an ideal pet. Pick up the kitten that you fancy. It may claw you and hold onto you briefly, but its initial fear and surprise should wane as you pet and reassure it. Does it respond or is it still unrelaxed, clinging, rigid with fear? A very young kitten, three or four weeks of age, will behave this way, and it is too young to take as a pet anyway. An older kitten behaving this way might not have had sufficient human contact, or it may be innately timid and fearful. It would be a risk to take an older kitten like this, especially if it failed the next test.

In a quiet room, where there are no other cats to distract it, put the kitten down. It might momentarily freeze and then cautiously sniff and explore. If it continues to freeze, it is too timid and may require a lot of work to come out of its shell. I would not take as a pet one that reacted this way. Call the kitten and try to get it to follow you. Young kittens have a good following response (see Figure 18, Chapter 5) and this should be strong. If it is weak or if the kitten completely ignores you, it may be too late to socialize it, and it may well remain aloof and distant toward people for the rest of its life.

A good test is to determine the readiness of the kitten to play. Will it chase a ball of paper or knotted piece of string? Unresponsiveness may indicate timidity. The kitten may be put off if these tests are done in a strange place, so it is advisable to give it a little time to explore and to get its bearings before you evaluate its temperament. The final test is to clap your hands loudly and shout at the kitten for five to ten seconds. If it scurries away and hides or freezes and then doesn't snap out of it quickly when you coax it to come to you, choose another kitten, especially if you are looking for a kitten that is going to live in a noisy house full of children.

When you get home with the kitten of your choice, again give him time to get used to the new place. Open up all the rooms and let him explore. If there are kids in the house, make sure they go outside if they can't keep quiet for an hour or so. Show the kitten where its litter tray is, and its food and water. It will miss its mother and may cry for a day or so. One can take advantage of this and give the kitten a lot of petting, thus effecting a transference of its need for mother to a need for its owner. This is the primary step in socializing the kitten. If there are no objections (and no fleas), there is no reason why a young kitten should not sleep in bed for the first few nights with its owners. Be sure to leave the bedroom door open so that it can get to its litter tray, though!

With a young kitten in the house it is important to walk differently. Don't pick your feet up in the usual way but walk in a sliding manner. This way you are less likely to crush your pet—a common tragedy in many homes. Also, children should be instructed how to hold the kitten. It should be held gently, but firmly, under the chest by one hand cupped under the chest holding the forelegs together and the other hand cupped under the kitten's tummy. A frightened or insecurely held kitten will squirm and claw. With young children, age three and up, get them to sit down first, since they will often drop the kitten the first time it struggles or accidentally claws them. In no time child and kitten will be together aware of each other's strengths and weaknesses, and sharing the joy of their own special world. With children under two years or so, the kitten and child may be in danger. Very young children have a "grab and hold" reaction which could frighten and even harm the kitten and result in a few deep scratches on the child. I have seen siblings almost pull a kitten in half, each child wanting the kitten for himself. Best then to get two kittens perhaps!

It is important never to disturb the kitten when it is eating or sleeping. Kittens need plenty of sleep, and excessive handling can be stressful. Always keep a new kitten indoors for four or five days so that it gets to know the house as its own place. It is less likely to get lost if and when it does get outside. Also, if you move to a new house, similarly keep your cat indoors for a few days before allowing it out. I am basically against letting cats roam free, and the reasons for this will be argued in Chapter 9. When you go on vacation, it is often less disturbing to leave the cat at home than to take it with you. (It may well get lost on the trip anyway.) Have a reliable neighbor come in and care for your cat each day. Cats are usually more disturbed by a change in their environment than by the absence of their owners. The reverse tends to be true for the dog. Consequently, putting a cat in a boarding kennel while you are away may be emotionally stressful and may make the cat more likely to pick up an infection while it is there. For the same reasons, prolonged hospitalization is to be avoided, and many veterinarians recognize this and avoid unnecessary hospitalization. Others make extra money out of this and should be professionally disciplined for such malpractice.

Having two kittens in the house does lead to a lot of fun and games, and it is good for the cats to have each other's company when the household is all out working and at school. For many solitary cats, an aquarium of fish or a bay window overlooking a bird feeder provides hours of entertainment. A kitten can also be a good companion for a dog and alleviate the neurosis of boredom and restraint when the dog is left alone (see *Understanding Your Dog*).

Introducing a kitten into a home where there is already a dog or cat can be a problem, though. The resident feels insecure and threatened by the newcomer, who is receiving all the attention. Jealousy, withdrawal, and even aggression toward the new kitten may erupt. My own son reacted this way when his little sister came home from the maternity ward. Fortunately, she survived and they are now as close as two peas in a pod. The trick was to make him feel secure and loved—lots of attention, treats, and so on. The same holds true for the resident dog or cat. With such a disruption in their lives, some cats may go off their food, stay in one room of the house and sulk and hiss for days (see Chapter 7). My parents' old terrier, after being restrained from killing a new kitten, sulked, went to his food bowl, and ate up all the dry chow. This soon developed into compulsive eating and we had to put him on a diet. Worse still, the kitten climbed into his sleeping basket. Somehow he managed to squeeze himself into her box, and he sat there, half in and half out, looking extremely depressed! In no time, though, they were playing together and would lie by the fire and gently lick each other. They both felt secure in each other's presence.

It is not necessary to overswaddle a kitten. A little stressful stimulation early in life can be beneficial for any infant, be it human, cat, or dog. Experiments with kittens, giving them extra handling each day for the first thirty days of life, produced "super kittens": Their eyes opened earlier than normal and their brain activity (EEG) matured faster. They were more sociable, more exploratory, less easily disturbed emotionally, and learned better in a number of problem-solving tasks. Similar experiments have been conducted on dogs by the author (see *Understanding Your Dog*). It is possible, then, with early handling, to improve the phenotype of an animal and to make it more resilient and adaptable as an adult.

If kittens are raised in a barren cage with no play objects or novel stimuli, they are less active, less inquisitive, and do not learn as well as kittens given an enriched cage full of toys and things to manipulate. As with dogs and children, then, early privation can have drastic effects on I.Q. and learning performance. A kitten should be exposed to a rich and varied environment early in life, otherwise it will be shy, withdrawn, will not explore new things and so will not learn anything new (see Figure 32). Such animal studies have emphasized the importance of providing optimal conditions for insuring that all potentials will be developed. Operation Head Start is as vital to humanity as is such early enrichment for a good cat- or dog-rearing establishment.

As emphasized in the preceding chapter, an important consequence of play is the development of social attachments. If kittens have no human contact during the first two or three months of life, they will be literally wild and impossible to handle. As in the dog, there seems to be a critical period early in life (ranging from four to eight weeks) when kittens are most easily socialized with people (see Figure 33). This attachment can be enhanced by giving the kitten a lot of handling (petting and stroking). Picking it up and holding it gets it used to being restrained. Encouraging it to play with you will help further to establish a close social bond. Petting during feeding has also been shown to make a kitten more responsive as an adult to its handler.

Kittens given frequent social experience (handling and play) with several different people from five to nine weeks of age showed less fear of strangers than those handled by only one person or not handled at all. The same rule for socializing pups, well documented in many studies, must therefore also hold true for kittens. If you want a cat to be socially well adjusted to people, it should meet many of them early in life. If it does not meet children, it will be shy of children when it matures. If the owners keep to themselves and have few visitors, the cat may also be less sociable. This is one of the ways, then, in which the pet *does* grow to be like its owner. A kitten

Figure 32. Well-adjusted kittens are highly inquisitive. A kitten responds to its mirror image and looks behind the mirror to find "the other cat" (this page). Another kitten responds to a sketch of a cat with vertical tail friendly approach and playful face-pawing (opposite)

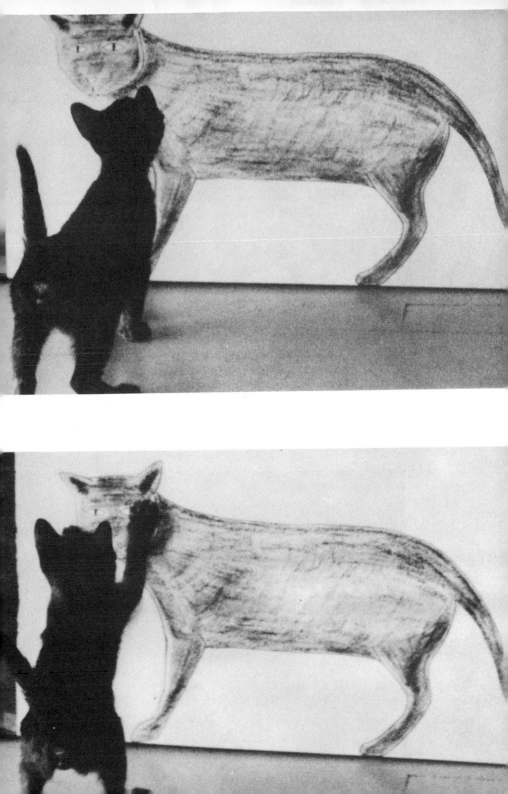

Figure 33. Reactions illustrating the process of socialization. An adult cat investigates a young kitten who approaches without fear. Its strange odor evokes a mild threat from the adult (above). Older kittens recognize a stranger and assume a defensive threat posture instead of approaching (below)

raised by a recluse will avoid strangers just as a dog will.

From one of my experiments one can draw obvious analogies with the concept and advantages of integrated schooling which optimizes socialization of children who are otherwise socioeconomically separated. Early socialization can facilitate later interactions: a litter of kittens raised with one Chihuahua pup grows up to be sociable toward other dogs, while most kittens that never meet a dog during their formative period are afraid of them (see Figure 34). Interestingly, a dog raised just with cats avoided interacting with dogs. The dog-raised cats had the best of both worlds and were socially more competent and adept at interacting with dogs.

The better socialized or attached a kitten is to its owner and family, the better a pet it will be. Avoid buying a kitten over twelve weeks of age from a large cattery if it has been raised with other cats and has had little human contact. Such a kitten usually grows up to be shy of people or aloof and difficult to handle. If a kitten is taken too young from the litter (say, at four or five weeks), it may suffer a temporary setback in growth since cats, nurse much longer than dogs. Worse still, such a kitten would not have had sufficient social experience with other cats. It may then become too human-oriented and overattached, which could lead to breeding and maternal problems later in life. Overhumanized cats can be extremely aggressive toward other cats, will often refuse to breed, and may refuse to care for their kittens. Without the feedback from other kittens during play, such a kitten may not learn to control its bite or sheath its claws when it plays with its owner.

Normally raised cats, weaned at eight or ten weeks and taken as pets at that age, still need some discipline when they bite too hard or get carried away play-fighting and rake your hand with their claws. Some will even attempt to nurse when they are being petted, the human armpit being a potent

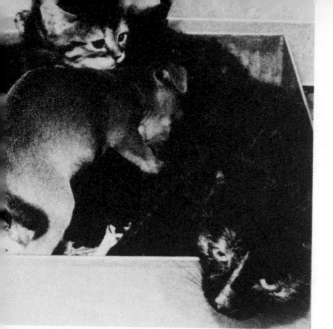

Figure 34. A mother cat readily accepts a 3-week-old Chihuahua pup.

As the pup matures, it becomes a socialized and integratal part of the litter.

releaser for this behavior. A standard disciplinary procedure for cats is to shout "No" and then give them a brisk flip with the hand on the nose (like mother cat who will cuff them on the nose with her paw). Soon the kitten will learn that "No" means to stop, and it will no longer be necessary to flip her nose. My own cats, trained this way early in life, will get down from a food-laden table or leave my dry grass arrangements and plants alone as soon as I shout "No!" In one experiment involving disciplinary training (where the cat must not eat until the signal is given), the training was retained into adulthood *only* if it was begun before the kittens were six weeks old. Training then must begin early.

Cats are trainable and extremely affectionate if they are socialized and raised correctly. Those who believe a cat to be distant and unsociable will raise them with these expectations, giving them little training or attention. No wonder their cats are distant and unsociable. Expectations about others (including cats) tend to be self-fulfilling prophecies!

Cats in the wild bury their feces and urine if they evacuate in their own territories, and this instinctive behavior makes the cat an ideal house pet. A kitten needs no training to use a litter tray. Just place it in the tray and leave him to it. If he does have an accident, place the droppings in the tray and show him again where the tray is. A newspaper advertisement of KITTENS FOR SALE, FULLY HOUSETRAINED is a come-on. No one trained the cat to be housebroken; all credit goes to instinct. It is unfortunate that the dog does not have this innate behavior in its repertoire. More will be said in Chapter 7 on emotional disturbances that can make a cat suddenly un-housebroken.

Long-haired Persian-type kittens should be trained to get used to being groomed as early as possible. Attempts to play, run off, or claw and bite should be disciplined in the same manner as outlined earlier. In addition, pick the kitten up afterward by its scruff and gently but firmly place it back on the table or floor and resume grooming. It is important that all cats, and especially long-haired cats, get frequent grooming especially in early summer, when they tend to shed more than ever. Grooming helps prevent fur balls. Many cats that groom themselves ball up a lot of fur on their rasp-covered tongues. These are swallowed and form large masses in the stomach, which lead to frequent bouts of nonproductive retching and loss of condition. A dose of mineral oil usually helps, or the cat herself will find and eat some grass in order to promote vomiting.* I have avoided referring to cat health and disease problems because this is not the purpose of this book, but a few remarks are warranted.

First is the disappointment of having a kitten die from feline distemper a few days after one has bought it from a pet store or humane shelter. Such places can be a constant source of disease to both dogs and cats. Although it is a kindness to adopt an orphan kitten from the shelter, *do be sure to have it examined by a veterinarian first.* A clean bill of health will not mean that it is not going to develop the disease a few days later. Ideally, go to a reputable pet store that offers some veterinary health certificate or insurance, or to a clean cattery run by a local breeder. Take your new kitten to the vet for the series of shots it must have to protect it from a number of killers, especially feline distemper (Panleucopenia), feline influenza, and feline pneumonitis. Kittens are also born with roundworms (the larval state of which passes across the placenta and infests the fetuses), and stool samples should be taken and the kitten wormed. Tapeworms (which cannot infest people) are common in cats, the commonest being contracted from dead rabbits and other wildlife your cat might

---

* Confined apartment cats should be given a little fresh grass occasionally; they seem to relish it as a tonic and in fact no flesh-eating carnivore eats meat exclusively. An all-meat diet can kill a cat.

eat, so prevent your cat's access to such a potential source of disease. Fleas may also carry the immature stage of a tapeworm which is very common in dogs (Dipylidium caninum), and it is advisable to frequently check your pets for fleas, especially in the summer months. Flea powder applied regularly is extremely effective. Flea collars also work, but they can make your pet sick and cause allergic reactions. Another common parasite in the cat is the ear mite which causes scratching *behind* the ear, and can also lead to severe bacterial infections of the ears.

An annoying behavior of cats is clawing drapes, furniture, and carpets. This is difficult to control even with training in some cats. A few will respond to a carpet-covered scratching post. Each time the kitten begins to claw the rug, pick it up and place it in front of its scratching post. Lift up its forelimbs and make scratching movements for it. The penny *might* drop, but often the cat will return to its favorite spots in the house and resume its clawing. With a persistent clawer, it is a simple procedure to trim the claws with nail clippers. Some cats will fight being restrained for this, and for some owners the only alternative is euthanasia. A third alternative is declawing, and although it is a controversial subject, I think it is better than getting rid of the pet because it persists in clawing furniture and scratching people. The declawing operation should be done but only by a licensed veterinarian. (I have heard of people using wire cutters and hacking off the cat's toes: a deplorable practice.) This is a skilled operation and is done under general anesthesia. Cats rarely suffer any psychological damage if the front claws are removed (I see no reason for removing the hind claws). They will continue to make clawing movements on furniture and rugs and otherwise behave quite normally after the operation. They should, of course, not be allowed out since they would be less able to defend themselves or to climb a tree in refuge from a neighborhood dog.

I also strongly urge owners to have their young cats spayed or castrated at five to six months of age. They do make better pets after the operation. A male no longer has the desire to go out every night and fight for his rights (vet bills for bite wounds and abscesses from deep wounds will be nonexistent too!). A castrated male is often more docile and less likely to spray and make the house smell. One of my cats, an Abyssinian, would attack visitors, and he once cornered his baby-sitter for a morning in a closet. Since he was castrated, such behavior has virtually disappeared. Spaying a female will eliminate the chaos that she might cause in the house when she is in heat. If castration is done too early, before four or five months of age, the growth of the penis may be arrested and this can lead to problems later in life. With a small penis, the urethra is too narrow to allow passage of small urinary calculi and an acute blockage may develop; surgery will be required to save the animal's life.

Although this book is not intended to provide first aid and veterinary advice for the cat owner,* there are a number of feline disorders that require neither surgery nor medication which are relevant to understanding your cat. These are emotional disorders and behavioral traits and abnormalities, some of which actually have their human counterparts. Sometimes, such anomalies are pronounced, resulting in some rather incredible case histories.

* See Chapter 9 for answers to some common veterinary and health queries about cats.

7

Behavior Disorders: Feline Fantasies and Neuroses

CATS GENERALLY SUFFER fewer emotional problems than dogs, probably because we have not domesticated them to the same degree of dependence. The late Fritz Perls, the noted psychiatrist and Gestalt psychologist, states that almost all human problems are based on one form of dependency hang-up or another. His therapy involves helping a person mature, grow up to be more self-reliant, independent, and responsible (and response-able) for his or her own actions. Perhaps this is why the cat is more immune than the dog to a variety of dependency-related disorders that may develop in the domestic environment.

But not all cats are immune. Perhaps because of their basic temperament and the way in which they were raised, some will develop behavioral abnormalities in this category of disorders. A change in social relationships, such as the death

149

of its owner, the introduction of another pet or a baby into the house, can bring on the abnormalities I will discuss shortly. First I will review some of the more common behavior problems and symptoms, recognition of which will enhance the owner's understanding of the cat and possibly make its life more agreeable.

Although cats are less affected than dogs by changes in interpersonal relationships in the home, they are generally more severely affected by a change in the environment. Cats seem to be more attached to a particular place and less to the people in it, while the reverse is true for the dog. Moving house, then, can be extremely traumatic for a cat. It may simply disappear, possibly trying to navigate its way home, which it may successfully do (see Chapter 4). Always keep the cat indoors for four or five days in the new house and give it lots of assurance and attention. Other symptoms shown by such displaced cats include depression, disinterest in food, defensive ragelike · reactions, and sudden lack of being housebroken. Some cats will stop grooming themselves, too.

The following case history * demonstrates very well the fact that a change in environment rather than in relationships can emotionally disturb a cat. This particular cat became unhousebroken, defecating all over the place, shortly after its owner got married. In many such cases, the cat is simply jealous, but in this instance a cure was effected by confining the cat to one room of the house (its favorite room before the marriage). When the furniture was put back, in this room, in the same way as it had been before the marriage the cat was content and no longer soiled the house!

---

* This and a number of other case histories described in this chapter are from the records of Dr. Ferdinand Brunner, a veterinarian from Austria, which he published in detail in my book *Abnormal Behavior in Animals*.

How do cats, with their rather poorly differentiated vocabulary, display embarrassment? One telltale sign is a brief bout of grooming. Cats will do it when they have been reprimanded for their actions and desires blocked by a command from the owner or by a hiss from a higher-ranking cat. Like an embarrassed person scratching himself or adjusting his clothing, a brief bout of grooming helps relieve tension. A cat that begins to wash and groom itself before a thunderstorm may, in fact, be nervous and apprehensive. Such actions are called displacements and are extremely common in mammals. Displacement paw-wiping has been seen in cats when a window or door is closed and they can't get out. A cat will often engage in displacement or *in vacuo* digging as though to cover up its food if, after eating, some food is left in its bowl. It will carefully paw the floor all around the bowl as if there were earth there to cover its food! Similarly, a cat will paw and earth-rake all around the *outside* of its litter tray if it has accidentally defecated on the edge or just outside the tray. The odor of feces triggers this action, which is automatically switched on and persists for some time, even though there is no earth on the floor to paw at. This is a rather comical superstitious kind of behavior that illustrates well how innate and fixed the hygienic action of the cat is. Next time you watch a late-night talk show host, switch off the sound and watch the variety of self-directed displacement behaviors he shows: wiping his eye, nose, smoothing his hair, straightening his tie, and adjusting other parts of his clothing. He is undoubtedly a seasoned performer, but at one time he may have been uptight and these actions most probably started then. They develop their own autonomy, though, and tend to persist indefinitely. In birds, displacement acts such as preening and ground pecking are actually inherited and have become incorporated into courtship rituals.

Boredom may cause a cat to groom excessively, which may lead to fur pulling and self-mutilation. This is not uncommon in cats confined for a period for boarding purposes and is very common in zoos. One case developed in a mountain lioness who was separated from her mate. She licked her flanks raw and did not stop until her mate was put back with her. Other cats will, under conditions of understimulation, or as a comforting displacement act, engage in self-sucking (see Figure 35). The flank, tail, a hind nipple, or a paw may be sucked.

Such nursing behavior is quite common in adult cats and can be a source of annoyance to the owner. The type of disciplinary training described in Chapter 8 should be employed to inhibit this behavior. I was asked what to do about this undesirable behavior by a veterinarian whose client had a Siamese cat that would attempt to nurse from anyone's armpit as soon as it got onto their laps. The vet tried to treat it himself, first by declawing the cat, then by removing its teeth! Doctors who care for humans often do little better; those with a penchant for surgery often use the knife before they use their heads.

Possibly related to this abnormal nursing behavior in adult cats is the predilection, especially in Siamese cats, for wool, which they will knead, suck, and chew. Serious complications from wool balls in the stomach may develop, as well as extensive damage to many garments. Possibly the lanolin in the wool has an odor not unlike that which is around the mother's nipple and acts as a chemical releaser, triggering nursing and even eating. The disciplinary training procedure outlined in Chapter 8 is effective in such cases.

Unlike dogs, cats rarely develop depraved appetites; I have never heard of a cat eating its own feces. Both cats and dogs will eat grass, though, possibly as a tonic or to promote

Figure 35. A cat engaging in self-sucking, an abnormal behavior in which it would always engage before going to sleep

vomiting. Dr. R. F. Ewer in her book *Ethology of Mammals* reports seeing young kittens regularly eating earth around the time of weaning. She regards this not as a perversion but as a highly beneficial action that may help populate the gut flora with bacterial organisms vital for digestion.

Cats have extremely sensitive nervous systems and often overreact to sudden and unexpected stimuli. A shock reaction may follow, as after a severe fight or narrow escape from a dog or automobile. Symptoms include depression and listlessness, disinterest in food, eversion of third eyelid, and rapid pulse. Panting, salivation, and sweating from the footpads may also be seen. The cat may hide, appear shy; it may shiver, show hyperesthesia (hypersensitivity to touch), and pupil dilation. If left alone, cats will often recover uneventfully, but in more severe shock reactions veterinary help may be needed. Sometimes a phobia may develop after such a reaction and the cat may persist in hiding and not venture out; gentle handling and reassurance is necessary and sometimes treatment with a tranquilizer is indicated. During the bombing raids in England during the Second World War, such shock or fright reactions were extremely common. After a severe coastal flood in one resort area in England, several cats showed this shock reaction, and, in addition, some developed a bizarre behavioral disturbance characterized by continuous and repeated attempts to catch imaginary objects both in the air and on the ground! Many of Pavlov's dogs, after the great Leningrad flood, also developed some rather unusual "neurotic" reactions.

Allied to the shock reaction is collapse and sudden death, which is not uncommon in high-strung cats. Restraint during routine veterinary examination or for anesthesia can cause this vasovagal attack, especially in Siamese cats. Careful

154

premedication with a mild tranquilizer prior to examination or administration of anesthesia can sometimes help avert such catastrophes.

An alarmed or surprised cat may occasionally become catatonic. This state of tonic immobility, or "sham death" (like playing possum), has been described in a number of animals, including the fox, rabbit, and deer; it is extremely rare in the dog. The significance of this behavior is not fully understood, but it may help some animals evade being chased and killed by a larger predator. Lack of movement stops the chase response and may inhibit the attack.

Like a dog, but more rarely, a cat may deliberately defecate or urinate shortly after it has been disciplined. It may also deliberately knock over ornaments; one of my cats used to do this at weekends when I would try to have an extra hour or so in bed and he wanted his breakfast!

Cats may react to a visitor (animal or human) as though its territory were being violated, much in the same way as a dog. It may attack or threaten the intruder, spray various objects in the house (or the stranger's overnight bag!), temporarily go off its food or even leave home. Castration may help reduce such reactions in mature cats. Comparable reactions may develop, not as a consequence of the animal's territory being invaded but because the cat is jealous (see later). If such is the case, extra attention and indulgence may do the trick.

A few abnormalities in sexual behavior and problems associated with occasional pseudo or phantom pregnancies have been discussed in Chapter 7. Pseudopregnant farm cats have been known to "adopt" a chicken or duckling. The hormones that turn on maternal responses seem to have an inhibitory effect on prey killing. Perhaps this is why a naïve carnivore mother does not immediately kill her offspring, which look more like prey than her own kind. A pseudopregnant farm dog would bring home and adopt baby rabbits: Before this time she would hunt and kill them.

Cannibalism of offspring is rarer in the cat than in the dog. The cause may well be owing to an incomplete hormonal inhibition of prey killing. In other cases, it may be owing to excessive outside disturbances at the time of parturition or as a consequence of aggression being redirected to the kittens after the mother has been disturbed and frightened or threatened by another cat. Two mother cats may take turns nursing each other's kittens, or the dominant cat may steal and adopt the subordinate offspring. If the other mother cat is her daughter, she may allow her to nurse!

Some cats do become extremely restless and even hysterical shortly before parturition. Gentle handling, reassurance, and sometimes light tranquilizing will help. Overdependent dogs often experience difficulties at parturition and will often refuse to have anything to do with their pups. Such reactions are extremely rare in the cat, probably because they have not been too domesticated and made so dependent as the dog. A disturbed mother may carry her kittens about from place to place excessively or groom them too much, to the point of mutilation. In such cases, a causal element should be looked for; the cat may not have a safe and quiet nesting spot, or a rival cat in the house may be disturbing her.

Sexual frustration, as a consequence of confinement in the house, can lead to increased restlessness, loss of condition, and increased aggression in both male and female cats. Chronic diarrhea may also develop, and epilepticlike seizures have been reported in some cats. Sterilization is the kindest and most effective treatment. Cystic ovaries is a common cause of repeated heats and "nymphomania"; the treatment is to remove the ovaries. Psychological castration is not uncommon in males. A known breeder may suddenly show no interest in females after experiencing a fall in social rank with the introduction of a more assertive tom into the household.

For many behavior disorders in cats, treatment usually involves careful handling, retraining, desensitizing, and occasional use of tranquilizers. Antibiotics and steroids are needed to protect an animal from disease that it might contract since resistance is lowered during emotional stress. The most dramatic case of drug therapy was reported by a veterinarian who had a Siamese cat brought in for euthanasia by its owner, since it was very wild and aggressive. He decided to use it as a blood donor, and after the third deep anesthetization with barbiturate (which was given in order that blood could be collected), the cat showed a complete change in behavior it was friendly and tractable. The effectiveness of deep anesthesia and handling under the drug might be explored further as a possible last chance treatment for such cases.

One particular case history of abnormal maternal behavior will introduce the final category of behavioral anomalies alluded to at the beginning of this chapter, namely those related to dependency and changes in interpersonal relationships.

Professor Blin and Professor Faveau from the Alfort Veterinary College in Paris had a female cat that became increasingly morose and aggressive and ultimately even killed her own kittens. Before these symptoms developed, the cat had been very indulged and was always the center of attention. It was discovered that her change in disposition began when her owners started to show interest in some of her earlier offspring. She became harder to handle, didn't groom herself, and was off her food and was increasingly ignored by the family. A vicious cycle therefore developed; no one wanted to pet an unkempt and aggressive cat, but the cat craved attention. The cure was to give it just that, and within a few days she made a complete recovery!

Fernand Méry in his cat book describes a case of mourning sickness in a cat named Fripon. This cat reacted violently to its mistress' death (she was laid out in her bedroom for a few days). Fripon stayed at her bedside and would go into a frenzy if anyone came near. She followed the funeral cortege to the cemetery and would go with her master every Sunday to visit the grave. Later she went daily by herself to lie by the graveside for a while. There is a statue of a dog in Edinburgh—Blackfriar's Bobby—who likewise visited his master's grave for some fourteen years!

Symptoms resembling shock reaction developed in a cat shortly after its owner died. Depression and refusal to eat food are not uncommon "bereavement" reactions and are especially common when the cat is left in a boarding facility or the owners go on vacation. (Under such emotional and physiological stress the cat is also more prone to develop an infectious disease.)

Extreme aggression has been seen in one cat toward other members of the household after its master died; another began defecating and urinating everywhere except in its litter tray! Refusal to eat and loss of being housebroken are the two cardinal signs of an emotional disturbance in cats, occurring frequently when the owners leave the cat at home in the care of a neighbor when they go on vacation. Another reason for this is the intrusion of a stranger—another animal or person. The resident may be marking its own territory (often the whole house!) with feces and urine. Apparently wildcats will bury their urine and feces within their territories but will leave their excrement exposed as a mark at the very edge of their territories. This helps explain the reaction of cats to intruders

158

when they suddenly cease to be housebroken. (As emphasized earlier, defecation and/or urination also occurs when a cat is frustrated by being reprimanded or not being allowed outdoors.)

As a final note, I must mention a number of psychosomatic disorders that may develop under a variety of emotionally stressful conditions in the cat. It is important to recognize that emotional stress may bring on clinical symptoms that appear to be those of a disease but, in fact, have no organic cause; the cause is purely psychological. Psychosomatic reactions to a broad spectrum of causes (jealousy at birth of a child or introduction of a new pet, sudden psychological trauma from being chased by a dog, etc.) include: diarrhea, vomiting, and pyloric spasms; gastric and duodenal ulcers; paralysis of the *membrana nictitans;* hypersensitivity to touch, twitching, and mild seizurelike movements; *anorexia nervosa* (refusal to eat); loss of hair. This clinical evidence destroys any criticisms of being overanthropomorphic about the emotions, needs, and reactions of the domestic cat. As emphasized in Chapter 3, the cat has the brain structures capable of reacting to similar stressors that affect man, and it will often respond symptomatically in a way identical to that of a human being.

Are cats over the next few years likely to develop more "neuroses" and emotional disorders as our life-style puts more pressure and demands on them? It is obvious that the cat, in coming close to man, is exposed to the same conditions that can cause mental health problems in man, and occasionally the cat succumbs, too. Is the cat more adaptable than man, and what does the future hold for man and cat?

8

Cat-People and People-Cats: Their Needs and Relationships

MAN HAS VIRTUALLY made the dog in his own image. The contemporary dog is extremely dependent, and, therefore, being willing to please its master, it is highly trainable. The dog also has many roles and fulfills many needs. Not only the traits that make them useful as companions or guards, but the almost pathological dependency of some dogs make them ideal child substitutes for young and old alike. (In a sense, such dogs are helping control the human population.) Such dependency, though, is the source of the many neuroses and emotional disorders so common in dogs today.

Dogs can also satisfy other human needs; a rare breed gives the owner status and identity; a graceful dog like a Saluki or a powerful mastiff can be a projection of the owner, accentuating her grace, his "gay" femininity, or the owner's aggressiveness. Conversely, the same dogs can fulfill introjected rather than projected needs. Thus a Saluki makes an ungainly person feel more graceful, and a mastiff gives a sense of power and strength to the insecure. In contrast to the dog, to what extent does the cat serve as "therapist" or emotional crutch for modern man? Can it also be an outlet for socially repressed, frustrated, or unfulfilled needs and desires? Do the projections, introjections, and expectations that some impose on their cats contribute to the development of some of the disorders described in the preceding chapter? Also, to what extent do the restrictions imposed on us in adapting to crowded urban living affect the cat? Is "future shock" acting upon the cat as it is on man and dog (see *Understanding Your Dog*)? Is the cat still a free, wild spirit in our midst, or must the cat, like its master, forgo many of its desires in order to belong and be accepted into home and society respectively?

These are not simply rhetorical questions to tease the intellect and imagination. For me they represent some key issues that concern the future of humanity, the quality and humaneness of life today, and the welfare of the pets, cat and dog, that we take with us. Life today, with its rapid rate of change—"progress and development," the credo of *Homo technos*—is a prime cause of insecurity. In a constantly changing world, how can one keep a sense of identity and equilibrium? Must we all become future-oriented and not live in the "now," or do we tenaciously hold onto the past, like a security blanket? A constant element for most of us is our home, not our children, for they soon grow up and leave. But the home may be temporary, since we expect our work to move us somewhere else or we hope to "move up" into a more expensive district. Few people today have neighborhoods that give them a sense of togetherness and place-identity; many live in anonymous bedroom suburbs or in housing developments where families are constantly moving in and out. A sense of impermanence confounds the modern scene—transience, anonymity, and loneliness. Material objects—a car (or two), as well as a house and other possessions—help some find a false sense of security and identity. For many, the one constant element in their lives must surely be their pets. It is always accepting; it is rarely if ever "moody" and can never change its values or attitudes, as so many friends, lovers, and colleagues do. It is a source of companionship, something to come home to for the young bachelor man or woman or the retired widower or lonely widow. It is often the one constant refuge and confidant for the child who may be ignored by indifferent parents or misunderstood because of his own inability to communicate. The pet makes no demands on him, whereas his parents do. He can't discipline his parents, but he can boss the dog or cuddle with the cat and feel reassured and loved. Life without pets today would be unimaginable, since they do play so many different roles for which it would be difficult to find any effective substitutes.

In order to "belong" to a particular socioeconomic class, to be accepted, one has to *conform*. This is one of the most powerful and often coercive if not corruptive pressures that man has had to deal with since he first became civilized. It creates a schism (the schizophrenia) between self and others, between one's own needs and beliefs and those of society. Often it is advantageous to forgo some egocentric, self-centered desires for the benefits of belonging and being accepted. It is a kind of trade-off, a compromise of one's freedom for the advantages that can be gained through conforming. For some, too much may be compromised and they become prisoners of conformity, giving up their own desires and beliefs for consensus. They may even be controlled by political and corporate voices that tell them what to believe, what to do, what to buy, own, possess, and even eat. Humanistic psychologists refer to such a human condition as being "other-directed" (*i.e.,* governed by others, so that one acts, feels, and believes as one thinks others expect he should). In contrast, an "inner-directed" person is one who is relatively nonconformist. Although he cares for others, he acts, feels, and believes from and for himself, although, on the "surface," he may appear to conform. The more dependent a person is, the more other-directed he is; he is also less responsible for his own actions. There are cultural differences, too—Americans tend to be more other-directed than Europeans. Ideally, there should be a balance between the two, the person being neither too conformist nor too self-centered.

I see the dog as other-directed, always willing to please its master at all costs, while the cat is the individualist, the nonconformist that shows affection when it feels like it. Few cats will use affection to "manipulate" others, while dogs and people certainly do. Is this one reason why some people prefer dogs and detest cats, while others much prefer cats? Do they identify something in their own nature that finds kinship or affinity with the dog or cat archetype? Others may base their preference not on an affinity with their own state of inner- or other-directedness, but rather to compensate for their own weaknesses or disequilibrium between self and others. A strong-willed, extremely inner-directed person may like to have a dog to boss around and to subordinate; he wouldn't have a chance with a cat or another strongly inner-directed person! His wife (or her husband) might well be a "dog," bending to his every whim and fancy. What of an excessively other-directed person? He may get much satisfaction from a cat companion, identifying closely his needs with the freedom and independence that his pet radiates. He may also enjoy a dog for two reasons. First, the dog may "suck," like the overdependent pet that he can overindulge; the owner literally places his whole life at home at the service of his demanding pet. A frustrated person who is forced by others to conform and who is by circumstance obliged to be directed by others may find solace in a cat or a dog. Again the archetype may radiate the feelings of freedom and independence that he is lacking. Or the dog may be a whipping boy for him to dominate and vent his spleen on; many dogs (and spouses) are used to release such pent-up, repressed feelings.

Having a cat as a pet can give one an anchor on reality in a world imploding with future shock. It can act as a link with nature, with the natural world from which we are separated by our highly technologized urban culture. The monstrous impersonal sameness of the urban scene replaces the diverse suprapersonal oneness of the natural world of wilderness, desert, and forest. Why else do people in the great cities of the world still keep pets in their cramped apartments, where space is a priority? Space alone is not enough, even in a crowded environment. Companionship and the link with a world that is not all man-made and man-controlled are important needs that a pet can partially fulfill. For some, one cat or dog is not enough; they need four or five, and when they come home, they have a "pack" of animals to greet them and a whole social system in which they have a meaningful role. Why else should a young woman in Brooklyn have five German shepherds and an old widow in Greenwich Village have twenty cats? They are not only giving refuge and love to unwanted pets, they are providing themselves with an animal world that gives them refuge and sustenance against the arid unreal world outside.

Many people go one step further (or "beyond") and take a wild animal as a pet—an even more authentic link with nature. There are "pet" raccoons, ocelots, cheetahs, lions, wolves, and monkeys all over the country, often kept in small apartments or in duplex basements. Tragically few of these animals adapt to such conditions, and state laws should be set up to ban the sale of any wild animal (even if it has been born in captivity) for "pet" purposes. There is nothing better than a cat or dog as a pet, not in terms of fulfilling one's need to have something real and wild like a wolf or a lion in the home, but rather in terms of their adaptability. Cats and dogs are more reliable and predictable (in the home with people) than any wild animal and adapt far better to "captivity" or the confinement that is the necessary imposition of modern life. But in adapting, sometimes too well, the dog and cat may acquire bizarre habits and other compensations in order to live close to its owner, but far from nature.

Many dogs and cats today will refuse to eat anything but their gourmet canned pet food or the best quality table scraps. A dog would turn up his nose at venison, which his cousin the wolf relishes, and a cat might well reject a fresh, uncooked fish or rabbit that any wildcat would enjoy. Likewise, modern man, accustomed to a diet of steak, corn, and potatoes, may have an aversion to fish or antelope and not know that in the wilderness he is surrounded by nutritious foods—berries, roots, wood grubs, ants, and grasshoppers, to name but a few. Our culture determines not only what we prefer but also, more generally, influences how and what we perceive. A totally enculturated man could die of starvation surrounded by a virtual banquet of items he no longer recognizes as food. Similarly, our dogs and cats become conditioned, early in life, to expect a particular type of food: This is a kind of food imprinting, a very fixed attachment. Some pets may almost die when it is necessary to put them on a special diet because they refuse to eat anything except what they are used to.

Being civilized, for man, and being domesticated, for the cat, entail many impositions or restrictions on doing what comes naturally. Social codes impose limits on what we can or cannot do and we similarly impose limitations on our pets. If we do not conform, we are ostracized, fined, or even imprisoned. If a cat does not conform, it is put to sleep. In the process of adapting to such pressures, both man and cat can suffer from basic needs being repressed or frustrated. As emphasized earlier, man does have some choice as to how far he wants to compromise himself vis-à-vis inner- versus other-directed urges and forces. But the cat has little choice. How can we help it adapt better? A cat whose prey-catching and killing instincts are blocked because it is never allowed out, may begin to attack its owners. The ankles of those passing by the cat waiting in ambush by the sofa become the necks of the prey he would normally attack. The same pent-up drive in the dog leads to car and bicycle chasing and even to chasing and nipping children that run by. Effective "therapy" for some cats is the provision of suitable play objects that resemble live prey—a furry toy, a clockwork or catnip-filled mouse; others will be satisfied periodically only with live mice. Man was also at one time a hunter, and the activity of hunting, killing, and bringing home a trophy is bound to the male ego. Such instincts are not lost in a contemporary man who likes to "make a killing" over a business deal, has to "hunt" for a job, or for clients (would-be prey?), and the trophy he brings home is a paycheck. Take these away, and his sense of worth, of pride, and of purpose are diminished, his ego is crushed. Success boosts the ego; failure destroys the man who has let his ego become his identity and who has fallen into the trap of valuing the things that he does above what he is. His role has become his identity; take away his role (his job) and he is nothing.

But men today still hunt, few for food, most for "sport," for ego. It is man's ego that destroys the wilderness, conserves animals not for their own sake but for his own uses, and transforms the ecosphere into a global egosphere. Cynics say it is better for some to vent their frustrations on killing animals rather than each other, and this may well be true in a number of socioeconomically deprived rural areas where prejudice and lack of opportunity and alternatives for changing the life-style are the catalysts to violence.

Man is not innately aggressive as a number of ethologists, such as Konrad Lorenz, might believe. *How* he fights may well be innate, but *who* he fights is determined by experience. Aggression is a survival action, released when other basic drives and needs are blocked or frustrated—such as sex, identity and status, belonging, and freedom from repression (benevolent or otherwise), or from being misjudged and discriminated against by others.

Similarly, the cat will aggress if some of its basic needs are blocked. A male cat, confined from roaming, may suddenly and viciously attack its owner. A jealous cat, feeling rejected by its owners because of a new kitten in the house, may try to kill it.

If cats are to live in relative harmony with us, we can help them adapt to some of the impositions we must impose on them by castrating them. This will reduce aggression and eliminate the sex drive.

Another aspect of behavior common to man and cat is territoriality. Man has had laws to protect his territory since the beginning of recorded history. No matter how poor, a man's home is his castle and this may be respected by all comers. With an increase in population, be it in an animal or human community, there is increasing competition for living space. This creates considerable stress and is further aggravated by the paranoid behavior of those who have territory (or "real estate") who feel that it is imperative to defend it against intruders. A man will put up a high fence and post "No Trespassing" signs. A cat will prowl and spray to mark his territory at a greater frequency if a rival is nearby; it may become so aroused as to spray inside the house and even attack visitors at the same time its master may bug the house with burglar alarms and purchase a firearm.

Paradoxically, a man will deodorize himself before going out in order to give himself a low profile in public. By reducing his personal identity in this way, as well as by wearing the anonymous gray flannel suit uniform, he likewise reduces the impact of interaction stress in a crowded urban environment. Similarly, a male cat must not leave his identity in the house, although it is natural for him to do so. Visitors might be offended by such an all-pervading odor; and before the guests arrive, the hostess sprays her armpits and also the place the cat has marked in the house—all is hidden by springtime lemon for the guests' arrival!

As a child, I was always taught to be civil to adults and put on a friendly air even when I wanted to be left to myself. Later I learned to play the role and assume a mask of overt friendliness. Likewise, we expect our pets to be friendly to all visitors, who may take it as a personal affront if the pet ignores them.

It is still acceptable for a cat to ignore visitors but not so for the dog, who may be even forcibly dragged over to "meet" the guests. Cats often like to be left alone, and many owners presume too much on the animal's need for privacy, cornering it, picking it up, and petting it even though it clearly wants to get away. The more we accept our pets (and other people) on their own terms, instead of imposing our expectations and values on them, the more comfortable the world will be.

Consider the neighbor who wants to shoot my friend's dog, who tore off a piece of meat from a deer he had shot and left out on his back porch. Why does another person put out strychnine-loaded bait to kill neighbors' cats who kill wild birds sometimes in her garden? To expect a dog not to scavenge a free meal once in a while or a cat not to follow its natural instincts is ludicrous, but it is a common attitude held by many. We cannot hope for our animals to live up to the expectations of others, but through selective breeding our domestic animals do in part satisfy such demands. Many dogs now readily accept strangers, while it is natural for a wild canid to avoid them. Many cats show no interest in hunting; this may be partly genetic but is probably owing to lack of appropriate experiences early in life. The same holds true for the dog.

In general, though, we cannot expect animals to behave *contra naturam,* to not follow their natural instincts. They cannot sublimate their desires, like man, although they can, like man, redirect to substitute objects. So a cat may be content to prey-kill a fluffy toy, or a tomcat will masturbate on a cushion. Many animals and people are less fortunate in that such outlets are unsatisfactory, and then the problems of frustration and repression discussed earlier arise.

For man, the basic issue of a person being responsible for his or her own actions is vital for the continuance of harmonious and productive relationships with others. We impose such values on our animals too, yet how can we expect an animal to show such responsibility? Admittedly, a dog will look guilty when you come home and you know at once he has done something wrong—eaten the roast or torn up a carpet. Such a capacity in an animal is remarkable. It would seem to be almost absent in the cat; few will show guilt the same way as a dog. Some of my cats will show a fleeting "anxiety-submission" when they have just done something wrong, but they will soon forget and will even go back and repeat the misdemeanor. A dog, in contrast, will react for hours and show true guilt and remorse. But can we condition a cat to feel guilty about spraying in the home, killing birds, or bringing home live prey (as a tribute to the owner or displaced maternal behavior of providing prey for nonexistent kittens)? Would it not be inhumane to instill a sense of guilt for what is natural for the animal to do? We do the same to children, and this accounts for many minor neuroses and unresolved conflicts in adulthood.

Fortunately, cats are almost out of the reach of such programming, and the question of responsibility then rests with the owner. In most places today it is ecologically a crime to allow a cat out to kill birds and other wildlife. Owners of dogs and cats also have a social responsibility to leash or otherwise restrain their pets to prevent them from roaming freely. Free-roaming pets can contribute to the spread of disease and contribute significantly to automobile accidents. A farmer would never think of allowing his cattle to roam onto the highway or down the village street. Owners of pets must assume the same responsibility for their animals, too.

Another serious breach of responsibility comes from people allowing their pets to roam and breed. There are too many unwanted pets anyway, so why aggravate the problem further by allowing your own pet to breed? Some justify this by saying it would be educational for the children to see their cat give birth and raise a litter of kittens. Others use their pet vicariously because they are either impotent or do not intend to have children themselves. As emphasized earlier, a spayed or castrated cat does make a better pet; perhaps only licensed breeders should be allowed to have fertile animals. How else can the pet-population crisis be rectified, since people in general refuse to accept the full responsibilities entailed in having a pet today? Twenty years ago there was no problem, but today there are more people and more pets and we have to face up to these contemporary problems and not dismiss them with the belief that they will be solved by someone else. The "someone else" may well be rigid law enforcements controlling pet ownership indiscriminately, a state that smacks of fascism, but which is inevitable in our "democratic" society, since so many people seem to be irresponsible, uninvolved, and socially uncommitted.

One of the main reasons why people lose interest in their pet is that it not only requires attention and restraint but also grows up. A kitten remains appealing and evokes much attention and affection until it matures. Its demeanor changes; it is less playful and entertaining; its body changes, the more mature conformation evoking fewer feelings of affection and tender loving care than a round-headed, big-eyed fluffy kitten. So the adult is given less attention and may be virtually ignored, if not neglected. It is allowed to roam free, and if it never returns home, it may not even be missed. Thus irresponsibility arises from people becoming disenchanted with their kitten as it becomes a cat. Cats are less fortunate than dogs in this respect since some dogs literally never mature. These are the "perpetual puppies" described in *Understanding Your Dog*, the best examples of which are some toy breeds like the poodle and Yorkie, which are genetically more neotenic (infantile) than many other breeds.

We raise boys to be boys and girls to be girls. From an early age, children of our sexist culture are stereotyped and pigeonholed into sex-related roles. Girls are raised with and reinforced by a set of expectations from parents and others, as are boys. In a similar way some people will raise cats one way, with one set of expectations, and dogs another. They think that a cat is aloof and distant, that it doesn't want much attention, so they don't try to leash-train it or engage in chasing or retrieving or wrestling games as they might with a dog.

172

If a dog is raised like a cat, it *will* be asocial and impossible to train. Give a kitten the same attention and training as you would a puppy and it will be a very different animal when it matures. No, it will not be a dog, nor will the little girl be a boy

For various reasons, I got my first cat several years ago. Igor was a Siamese, refreshing company after a day's work at the lab with dogs, and he didn't seem to mind being left alone while I was away at work. I raised him just as I would a puppy—trained him to come, fetch, and follow me on walks, and so on. We even engaged in stalking and rough-and-tumble games. In one game I would bite his paw gently and he would bite my nose gently. The harder I bit, the harder he would bite until I gave in. This was my first close relationship with a cat, much of which can be attributed to my rearing it without any particular expectations—simply trying out what felt best for both of us. Perhaps this is the best foundation for any relationship.

A final analogy pertains to the dilemma of modern man, which the cat has not had to face since it is basically a solitary or highly individualistic being. The cat, being a relatively solitary animal, is freed from the pressures of having to belong to a social group. Unlike dog or man, it does not have to be deferential and display submission to superiors. Nor does it get caught up in the bind of striving for acceptance, for status, or for power. It has been proposed that a basic cause of mental disease in man is rooted in the social hierarchy. Failure to achieve status causes frustration and aggression; a fall-off in status causes depression, while insecurity in one's social position or role leads to anxiety and paranoia. High status, on the other hand, can lead to megalomania. Much energy is wasted by people striving for status, success, and power; the more insecure a person is, the more he strives. Only in social groups of dogs, monkeys, and men do we see social outcasts (the pariahs of a community) and status rivalry and despots. The advantages of belonging to a group are not equal for all individuals since the best of animal and human societies are rarely wholly democratic. Caught in the bind of having to adapt to such pressures, an individual is inexorably involved, swept up into having to compete in the rat race. Survival itself seems to depend on status. Children in most schools today are encouraged not to cooperate and develop social skills but instead to learn to compete with one another from an early age and are rewarded for this. They will then be well equipped for the status struggles of adulthood.

Some educators are aware that they are conditioning children with really false attitudes and at the same time preparing many for a life of striving, dissatisfaction, and possible mental illness. Might as well teach a child how to compete if that's how it is in society anyway, is a common rationalization. Those with the strength, courage, and conviction to walk alone—like the cat—often find happiness and fulfillment in their lives. They are not dependent on the views or acceptance of others, and are not swept up in the rat race around them. To be ostracized and branded as radicals, eccentrics, social deviants, or whatever does not affect them, since they are not caught up in the mainstream of conformity or bound by the limiting conventions of a structured society. Conservative critics would claim that no society could exist without structure and rules; but structure and rules can inhibit growth and change. The rules of one generation can hold the next in limbo. Man is still evolving, and one must be optimistic that a more liberal and free-flowing social structure will eventually become global. Teilhard de Chardin, Jesuit, philosopher, and noted paleontologist, forsees man evolving toward such a global society, a true brotherhood of humanity. We have only just begun.

Man is caught in the double bind of being, like the cat,

highly individualistic, but at the same time a social animal with acquired social needs (*i.e.*, acceptance, recognition, status, success, and power). In order to fulfill his needs he must forgo something of his own individuality. Teilhard de Chardin is optimistic in this regard, in spite of the pessimistic views of R. D. Laing and other psychiatrists. They see man caught eternally in this double bind, which is the cause of so much mental sickness today. De Chardin holds that with greater involvement and "compressive socialization," man may not fear that he will lose his individuality in a collective and united society. Such a society "suprapersonalizes" the individual who essentially finds himself in others. This is far from the materialistic and mechanistic society of today, where people are computer punch-card numbers and are otherwise made into nonpersons by being stereotyped as "blacks," "students," "clients," "patients," "consumers," and so on.

We continue to evolve culturally and to grow personally, the two being reciprocally dependent. As we develop, our needs and values change. The uses that we make of our pets today differ from those of fifty years ago. It will be interesting to see what uses they serve and what values and expectations we have for them fifty years *from now*. We and our pets are evolving, civilization and domestication unfolding together. We and our pets have also changed significantly over the past ten thousand years, at which time man first began to domesticate animals. Domestication of the cat began several thousand years later than the dog, and, since then, changes wrought by selective breeding on the wild feline prototype have been minimal. Of all the cat breeds, the Siamese is perhaps the most "doglike"—more trainable and dependent than other breeds. Perhaps over the next few years other breeds of cat will be more like this in order to satisfy many of the human needs discussed in this chapter. The cat will then be more likely to be more susceptible to behavioral disorders.

The incidence of mental health problems in the human population is reflected in the pet population. It is hoped that this chapter will help offset some of these logical future expectations and also help in the recognition and alleviation of emotional disorders in cats today and tomorrow.

9

Cat Owners Ask Me

THE FOLLOWING SELECTION of questions and answers will help many readers with some of their individual cat problems. This material has been selected from the author's personal file and from his column "Ask the Vet," which appears monthly in *Family Health* magazine.

Why is a cat's tongue rough, like sandpaper?

A cat's tongue is rough for at least two reasons. The rasps on the tongue allow it to lick the bones of its prey clean of meat and especially enable it to groom itself thoroughly. Loose hair and debris are raked out with the tongue, while a dog uses its front incisors and nibbles and pulls. Since the rasplike papillae on the tongue point backward, hair is difficult to dislodge and it is easier for a cat to swallow its hair. This normally causes no problem, the hair being passed undigested in the feces. With long-haired varieties, and short-haired cats in summer molt or who molt constantly, balls of fur can aggregate in the stomach. Unless these are vomited, the cat will soon lose condition. Grass, to evoke vomiting, or a mild laxative such as mineral oil should be given.

How can I stop my cat from eating and mutilating my houseplants?

You might try a simple training procedure of shouting "No" at your cat any time you catch it chewing on one of your plants; immediately follow this loud exclamation by throwing something at it, like a dried pea. Keep a handful handy in conveniently placed bowls. Throwing anything within reach could damage both cat and plants! Your cat may well need some green in its diet and many people advisedly grow a box of greens for their cat if it never has a chance to get out and select grass for itself.

I think my cat is schizophrenic. She comes and sits on my lap all friendly and rolls over, but if I tickle her stomach she claws and bites and runs away. Is she crazy or what?

No, your cat is not schizophrenic. This is a common reaction in cats. Being tickled while lying on their backs seems to release defensive aggression. This is the normal position a cat assumes in order to defend itself against an adversary, and tickling it on the stomach could act like a reflex and switch on a sudden outburst of scratching and even biting.

Cat Owners Ask Me

Our cat got quite large after her heat and we thought she was going to have kittens. She's back to normal size and no kittens. What happened to them?

Two things could have happened. First, your cat was pregnant and the fetuses were reabsorbed into the uterus. The second possibility is that your cat had a false or pseudopregnancy. This is far more common in dogs, though. Some cats will even produce milk, choose a nesting corner somewhere in the house, and occasionally "adopt" a toy or suitable object and carry it around and protect it like a kitten.

Why are Siamese cats more like dogs than other cats? Mine will retrieve things and go on walks. Is is true that a cat can sometimes breed with small dogs?

There is no authenticated case of cat × dog hybrids, although many hoaxers have made such claims. A Siamese cat is more doglike than other varieties of cats mainly because of selective breeding. It is one of the most dependent breeds of cat and responds well to training and reward. They make excellent pets for those who would like to have a dog but for various reasons cannot, and have not had much experience with cats before. Unfortunately, Siamese cats are popular and are consequently highly inbred. Many have genetic defects— such as a severe disabling squint or skeletal disease *(osteogenesis imperfecta)*. Others have bad temperaments, either extremely timid or unpredictable and aggressive. Cats with such traits should not be bred, and, as in the case with many popular breeds of dog, rigorous culling of inferior individuals is essential.

179

Why does my cat sometimes bring home a bird or mouse she has killed and leave it on the kitchen step? Is it for me or what—she has no kittens?

A mother cat will bring home dead mice and other prey for her kittens, and when they are older even live or injured prey. This behavior of the mother insures that the kittens will learn early in life that dead prey means food. By observing and imitating their mother when she kills the live and injured prey, they also learn how to kill prey. Domestic animals often exhibit a hypertrophy or excessive discharge of certain inborn behaviors, one being bringing home live or dead prey. It is less a tribute or token offering to you than an instinct which, even in the absence of kittens, can persist. The most persistent and ingrained instincts are those associated with survival (*e.g.,* flight and attack), and certainly the provision of prey for weanling kittens fits into this category. In its absence, kittens in the wild would not survive.

Can cats swim? Mine watches me in the bathtub, and I'm sure he wants to join me, but he never dares!

Cats can swim. The bobcat is an excellent swimmer and young tigers enjoy a romp in a pool. Domestic cats, although good swimmers, naturally avoid getting wet. They do not have the same oily coat as a dog, and their coat lacks the film of guard hairs that tend to keep the soft, fluffy undercoat of the dog relatively dry when the animal is immersed for a short time.

My cat's favorite place, where she sits for hours, is on a win-

dowsill. Sometimes she gets excited, wags her tail, and makes a funny, chirping noise. Is she looking for other cats and should I get her one for company?

Your cat is most probably spotting a bird or even a fly high up on the windowpane. Tail wagging and the "chirruping" vocalization are usually given when a cat is aroused by the presence of prey, such as a mouse, bird, or flying insect.

My cat washes herself when I think she is embarrassed. Am I being too anthropomorphic or am I right?

No, you are not being too anthropomorphic. A cat will briefly wash itself when it is anxious, as before a thunderstorm or after being disciplined. This is a fidgety "displacement" activity, just as an uptight person adjusts his hair or clothing, wipes his nose or eye, or momentarily scratches himself!

Is it true that male calico cats are rare?

The gene for calico color usually occurs only in females. Male calico cats are extremely rare and they are usually sterile.

In addition to the two dogs that we have had for three years, we recently acquired a kitten. We have had the kitten for two months, introduced her slowly to the dogs, but we are still having major problems with our pets.

Our dogs generally stay out during the day, coming in only to sleep. Our Irish Setter is so afraid of the kitten that he will not settle down until she is locked in a room (which she dislikes). Our other dog presents an even greater problem. He urinates on things that she owns (like a box) and on pieces of furniture that she has been on. We have tried everything we can think of—from spankings (he growls) to extra love and attention. We do not want to keep our dogs out all night, nor do we want to lock up our kitten in a room. You touched on this subject recently in your column, but we have already tried the extra attention, to no avail.

Since we have had the problem for two months, and obviously the pets are not getting along well together, could you offer us a specific suggestion?

You certainly do have a problem! This is a complex situation to handle with two dogs reacting so very differently. I suggest you find a good home for the kitten rather than get into a very involved series of procedures to attempt to rectify things.

Is it absolutely necessary to spay a female house cat that will never be mated or stray outside? I don't want to put my cat through the operation unless she may develop tumors or related "female troubles" in later years.

No, it is not necessary to spay a house cat that always stays indoors. For some varieties, like Siamese, it is often advisable to spay if you don't intend to breed them since they can develop prolonged heat cycles. This is often referred to as nymphomania, the female having repeated heats and becoming an annoyance, pacing and rolling all the time and calling in a loud voice. It is perhaps a kindness, too, to prevent the cat from literally climbing the walls when she is horny!

Cat Owners Ask Me

Are white cats deaf? When my white cat was a young kitten, she seemed deaf. As she got older she did hear.

White-colored animals are often deaf. Sometimes a kitten doesn't respond to your voice and seems to be deaf. As it grows up, it learns to be more responsive, which is probably what happened in your case.

Recently our white pet cat vomited and died. It had not been sick before except for some vomiting about once a week. I did not take it seriously, and now people tell me an animal can suck the vomit back in its lungs.

Frequent vomiting is usually caused by fur balls in the stomach (a dose of mineral oil will help remove them). The probability of inhaling vomit and choking is very low. More likely your cat had an infection—feline distemper or infectious peritonitis—but it is now impossible to tell what your cat died of without an autopsy.

I have two Siamese cats from the same litter. Would it be safe, genetically, to let them mate? Their father is a blue point, their mother a seal point.

Siamese cats have many inherited abnormalities that are a consequence of excessive inbreeding. Although your cats may produce a normal litter, I would, in this breed, seriously reconsider any brother × sister mating.

I have a thirteen-year-old cat who has a sore on her stomach. It

183

heals up, then it breaks out again in little red spots. Is it cancer?

Your cat may be intermittently licking the area and preventing it from healing naturally. Sometimes an "Elizabethan collar" (a stiff plastic or cardboard lampshade attached to the animal's neck) is necessary to stop the animal from mutilating itself. A vet should take a look at the skin problem and prescribe the appropriate treatment.

In the past two days two of my three kittens died of distemper. The other kitten and the mother are all right—apparently treatment was started in time for them. What exactly is distemper, what are its characteristics, and what kind of treatment do you suggest?

Feline distemper, or panleukopenia, is caused by a virus that attacks the blood-forming system and causes leukopenia (lack of white cells). This increases susceptibility to bacterial infections, and cats die, not because of the virus itself but because of secondary infections. The virus can also attack the intestinal wall and cause severe enteritis. Kittens infected before birth *(in utero)* or shortly after birth may also develop brain infection, and nervous symptoms develop. Vaccines are available, but repeated vaccinations are necessary because the antibodies a kitten gets in the mother's milk actually interferes with the development of immunity.

I am having difficulties with my one-and-a-half-year-old Siamese cat. She is independent and not lovable. She does not want to scratch. How can I get her to do this? Also, I am unable to open my apartment door without her running out and up the stairs. How can I prevent this?

Why do you want your cat to scratch? Most people want to stop their cats from doing this! Cats do like to rush out as soon as the door is opened. Next time you open the door just a little, bend down, shout "No!" and flip your cat hard on the nose. A few repetitions of this should train her. Siamese, although independent, are often very receptive to training.

My female Manx cat eats only raw beef (not hamburger!) and loves cooked crab meat (at six dollars a pound!). During the day, she works over some Purina dry cat chow, too, and once in a while a raw egg yolk beat up in a little milk (plain milk she backs away from!). She also gets a vitamin pill a day. Is this sufficient to maintain her health?

If two-thirds of her diet is one of the major brands of chows (a balanced ration), all should be well with what you give your cat. A little fresh grass is a good "tonic," which many cats relish. Avoid giving her too much unbalanced food like meat, no more than one-third of her daily ration.

Our six-year-old cat is receiving one-fourth of a gram of phenobarbital daily for epilepsy. Her hair is falling out in clumps, and her skin is turning red and scaly. Is this related to the treatment?

It is unlikely. You might consider a dietary insufficiency, which would cause such a dermatitis. A skin scraping to test for mange may also help pinpoint the problem, although hormonal (especially thyroid) imbalance can cause dermatitis, as well as an allergy.

I have an active male tabby cat. He gets his kicks out of killing birds and rabbits whenever he is out. How can I stop him from doing this?

Your cat is doing what is natural for him, and the only thing you can do is to keep him confined indoors.

We have a six-year-old female tiger cat (who has been spayed). She was covered with a rash on her neck, chest, and back. Our vet prescribed cortisone and vitamins, which helped for a while, but the rash has come back. The vet refuses to prescribe more cortisone, saying it would be harmful for her. Can you recommend anything?

Your cat may have an allergy—to food, fleas, floor polish, any number of things. I suggest you consult your vet again. He is right—too much cortisone can be dangerous, but the problem clearly does need to be solved.

Do the hard foods, such as the major dry cat chows, produce cystitis in cats because of the high ash content? Ours love it, but because our male Siamese nearly died, I'm reluctant to give it to our cats. I believe they do need something other than soft food, if for no other reason than to aid their teeth. What do you suggest?

It is not really the diet that causes cystitis and calculi (stones) in castrated cats but, more probably, a metabolic anomaly that follows castration. In addition, the penis can be smaller so that small calculi cannot be voided. Cats also are prone to develop bladder infections, so don't blame the food. I have a castrated male Abyssinian—I give him Purina chow and every other day a moist canned food, table scraps (he loves corn on the cob and bananas), and grass (lawn, that is). Diversity of diet, but a balanced diet, is a safe rule.

How long does a chipmunk live? I am tired of being asked this as I don't know the answer. Chippy, our pet chipmunk, plays with the fifteen-year-old cat that brought her to us the first Sunday in May seven years ago. She eats about everything we do, plus the extras we buy for her, like sunflower seeds, walnut meats, etc. Besides her milk, she has her water bottle.

I have a graduate student completing her PhD on chipmunk behavior and ecology; they are fascinating animals, with a well-developed repertoire of communication signals and territorial property rights. Since they are preyed on by owls, stoats, foxes, and so on, they produce many young, but few survive longer than two or three years. Living for seven years in captivity must be a record.

As for your fifteen-year-old cat that brought the chipmunk home as an infant to play with, and still plays with it—it supports one of my main beliefs: Pets need pets, and provided no one is frustrated and deprived of security, food and affection, prey and predator, mouse and lion, can, and will, live peacefully together. This goes for man and animal, too. "We are all brothers; all is one," said the coyote to the Indian boy.

What are the effects of castration and spaying in cats and dogs?

Castration and spaying in cats and dogs have more or less the same effects as in people. A sexually experienced male cat or dog may still show sexual interest and the desire to roam, but many males and most females usually show a gradual decline in sexual behavior. With sexually experienced adult humans, there is an even lesser dependence on hormones. Sterilization early in life in all mammals, including man, invariably arrests all sexual behavior and influences growth and development of secondary sexual characteristics (pubic and facial hair, voice, etc.). I recommend operating on pets after their first heat. The operation is a kindness to male cats, whose gonads literally *make* them go out and fight. It is also a public and humane service, in view of all the unwanted pets that abound today.

Some people in my community are lobbying for an ordinance that requires cat owners to keep their pets on a leash. I think it is retaliation for a proposal requiring dog owners to clean up after their dogs. I contend nature didn't intend cats to be leashed. What do you think?

Twenty years ago, it was fine for dogs and cats to roam free in most places. But we have so many pets in populated areas today that some restraints are needed. Dogs obviously contribute to fecal pollution, but the cat problem is no less serious. With the proliferation of cats in recent years, the ecological impact on wild birds, to cite just one problem, must be tremendous. So, for health and ecological reasons, laws are required to restrain pets from following their natural instincts. True, few cats tolerate a leash, but remember most cats do well indoors and are spared the many dangers of roaming free— being run over by cars and picking up parasites, to name a couple.

Our cat appears healthy but is passing considerable amounts of blood in his stool. There isn't a veterinarian near us, so could you recommend some treatment?

You really should try to get him to a vet somehow. Passing fresh blood means that there is bleeding near the anus caused by an anal or rectal abnormality—a polyp, ulcer, cancer, warty growth, or congenital constriction that can cause constipation and, when he strains to evacuate, bleeding. As a temporary relief, feed him raw milk plus moist canned cat food to help loosen his bowels.

My cat drools constantly. I was told this is not natural. How can I prevent this drooling?

Cats often drool, particularly when they are relaxed and being petted. About all you can do is remind yourself that things could be worse—what if you had a drooling St. Bernard! Your cat could also have a rare neurological disorder, and a veterinary checkup might be advisable.

One of my cats—she's not pedigreed—has a tuft on each ear like a lynx. Could she have lynx blood or something?

I have seen many domestic cats with lynxlike ear tufts; the lynx and cat are in the same *Felidae* family, but the domestic cat is not derived from lynx. The tufts serve to enhance ear signals of threat and submission. Other felids like the tiger have a white eyespot on each ear that serves the same function.

My twelve-year-old calico cat had been breathing hard and fast

189

*for two or three days. I took her to my vet—she was purring so
hard and loud he could not examine her, so he shook her real
hard. That made her quit purring, and after listening to her
heart, he said there was nothing he could do for her but put her to
sleep. I left her there, and after hours of indecision, I finally
phoned him to go ahead and put her to sleep. I am now suffering
guilt pangs—if only he had not shaken her so hard—I feel she was
frightened and met a horrid end. Should I change vets?*

If I were the vet I would have had to do the same thing; you
cannot listen to a cat's heart and chest while it is purring. But
I would have asked you to leave the room first. Vets are very
busy and sometimes forget that some of the things they do
might offend and hurt a sensitive owner. Don't feel guilty—
both you and the vet did everything possible for your pet, who
had your affection while she lived. What more is there? Her
end was more traumatic for you than for her, I'm sure.

My cat eats grass. Is something wrong with her?

Probably not. Wild carnivores often eat the stomach contents of their prey first, and this consists of semidigested plant
materials—salad before the main course, a well-balanced
meal. Domesticated cats will settle for grass as a salad, and,
especially for cats confined to an apartment, this is a good,
natural tonic.

*I've heard some bad things about pets being shipped by air
freight. They are dead on arrival. This happened to one of my
friend's show dogs. They said he must have been ill before the
flight, but he was given a clean bill of health and a health permit
for shipment out of state by the vet. What can be done?*

190

Cat Owners Ask Me

On *some* airlines you can take your pet on board provided that it's no bigger than a toy poodle and has a suitable carrying case. Usually one animal—and no more than two—may be on board at the same time. The rest—and anything much bigger than a cat—must go in the baggage compartment. You can get courier service on some airlines and take your pet to the gate and avoid sending him through the baggage route.

But in the baggage compartment, which is supposedly pressurized and, according to most airlines, quite safe for your pets, death can strike. A recent *Consumer Reports* notes that temperatures can range from zero to 130°F., and that, since the hold is airtight, there will be little air for animals in transit if the compartment is filled with baggage.

Are the airlines guilty of misleading the public? (One airline's pamphlet on pets, given to consumers, states that the animals travel in "heated, pressurized comfort," just like you in air-conditioned aircraft.) *Consumer Reports* labels this as a "cruel deception." Is the increase in charges for shipping animals needed to defray payments to owners whose pets they killed? How can any airline company encourage pet owners to ship their animals by air in an environment that can kill from heat stroke, suffocation, or disease (pneumonia, enteritis) developed as a consequence of such transit stress?

The critical factor is not humane treatment but profits vs. losses—the almighty dollar. An air-conditioned baggage compartment would be costly. Why not a smaller, climate-controlled section for pets? And who will pay—the consumer, of course. Better the equivalent of a first-class ticket for your pet, though, than a dead cat at the end of the flight.

My cat has scratched itself bald behind the ears. I put salve on the bald spots, but it hasn't helped. Please advise.

191

It is usually no use treating the bald, scratched areas behind the ears. These tell you the cat has some irritation in the ears, and nine times out of ten it will be ear mites. These are extremely irritating, causing the ear glands to secrete excessive amounts of dark brown cerumen and often giving rise to secondary bacterial infection. Have a careful look inside the ears then and gently test inside with a Q-tip. If it comes out caked in cerumen, you can get appropriate medication from a good pet store, but, ideally, get a veterinarian to give your cat's ears a thorough examination and cleaning.

What is cat scratch fever? A friend of mine said she got it from her cat and was quite ill. Should I get rid of my two cats?

No, I do not advise you to get rid of your cats, even though they could give you cat scratch fever. This is an acute reaction to a scratch, where the lymph glands near the scratch become swollen and painful and the person experiences periodic episodes of nausea, fatigue, and fever. Hospitalization is sometimes indicated. More doctors are recognizing this disease now, which can be confused with lymphatic cancer (it is a leukemia-like disease). A cat breeder I know was greatly relieved when, just before a biopsy of one of her lymph glands was to be done, the doctor found out that she had cats and he put "two and two together." Cat scratch fever, not cancer!

This disease is not fatal, and there is a very low risk indeed that you will get it after being scratched. I feel that such low-level risks are offset by the many benefits and joys our feline companions provide us with. Extremists would have all cats destroyed and never go near a cat themselves. Do these same people walk to work, too, knowing that the dangers of driving a car are a millionfold higher?

Cat Owners Ask Me

This last fall my little girl was covered in spots. I thought it was chicken pox, but the doctor said it was fleas. We have a flea collar on the cat now. Will this be enough? Also, our cat is now being treated for tapeworms. Can these infect my child?

A flea collar is effective in keeping fleas off your pet, but it will soon lose its potency and should be replaced according to the manufacturer's instructions. Cat fleas lay their eggs, which drop off the cat and develop in nooks and crannies in the house. The eggs mature into fleas in about three weeks, and especially in the fall the population can reach an all-time high in your house. At such times, flea powder applied every ten days to your pet will help reduce the infestation.

Cat and dog fleas harbor the developing eggs of a tapeworm so that when the pet actually catches and eats one of the fleas on its body, it becomes infested by the worm. Segments of this worm, about the size of a grain of rice, which can move themselves independently, may be found in the feces of your pet or crawling in the fur around its hindquarters. Ask your veterinarian for a prescription since the tapeworms may make your cat quite ill.

If cats can be trained to use a litter box, why can't dogs?

It would save us a lot of trouble if dogs would use a litter box! You say cats must be trained, but this is not quite true. They will instinctively use a litter box even without prior experience as kittens. In nature, felines normally make a hole and bury their feces, while canids, members of the dog family, never bury their droppings. This is the reason then—cats do what comes naturally, and dogs cannot be trained to do what is unnatural or not within their normal behavior repertoire.

193

I have heard of spay clinics being set up in some cities for people who can't afford the high price of the operation for their pet. How can I find out more?

The Fund for Animals (140 West Fifty-seventh Street, New York City) is attempting to set up nationwide spay clinics for cats and dogs, where veterinarians will contribute their time and do the operations at a greatly reduced rate. They are aware of the severe overpopulation of unwanted pets, and this is a top-priority program. After publicly criticizing veterinarians for exorbitant fees for spaying, in a recent article in *Saturday Review/Science* (November, 1972), I have since received many strong letters of protest from aggrieved veterinarians. The point, however, is that spaying is no longer a cosmetic operation but one of great social and ecological importance. It was with great surprise I learned that in one of many states, Florida, local veterinary associations are putting pressure on a minority (0.001 percent) of their profession who are giving some of their time to help in the reduced-fee spaying program. They want them to stop. Price fixing is inevitable in any profession, and to be undercut hurts when spaying is the bread and butter income in a veterinary practice. They argue that a family that cannot afford to pay between fifty and a hundred dollars for the operation obviously cannot afford to keep a pet. This is irrational, and I, for one, hope that local veterinary associations will donate their time and support these spay clinics as they have done so admirably for rabies vaccination clinics. Some argue that such clinics will not have any significant effect on the population problem. A 5 percent decrease alone would be significant and would certainly lower the rate of suffering in unwanted and homeless animals.

Our cat had her first litter two months ago. When the kittens

194

were about four weeks old, she behaved as though she were starting to nurse them. We kept the kittens inside until they were five weeks old. If the kittens tried to nurse, the mother cat wanted to go outside. Was she trying to tell us she wanted the kittens outside with her or was she disowning them?

When the kittens were about seven weeks old, they wandered out of the yard with the mother. When we saw them later, the mother had caught a rabbit. She laid it down for the kittens and wouldn't eat a bit of it (even though she had eaten with the kittens before). The next day the mother wouldn't even go near the kittens—when she saw them coming she would get up and leave. Suddenly the kittens got weaker and weaker, and two days later all four kittens died. Our thought was that the rabbit had been poisoned and this killed the kittens. Did the mother ignore the kittens because she knew they were dying?

It sounds like your cat, right on schedule, was weaning the kittens. Often at five weeks, a mother will bring home dead prey (mice) and soon after "train" the kittens with live prey. Your cat gave them a rabbit and this was certainly weaning time, although kittens at this age still nurse from the mother. Perhaps she had no milk and couldn't provide the kits with sufficient food. They more likely died from an infection (like feline distemper) than from starvation (since she sounds like she was a good mother) or from a sick/poisoned rabbit.

We have always had a cat as a family pet, but our present one has a behavior we have not encountered before. At night she will go to bed early. When my wife goes to bed, she feeds the cat and closes the door to the room. Most always she will get up and have a snack and then hop back into her bed. I let the cat out of the room in the morning. Now the food plate is nearly always empty, and on top the cat has carried and placed her two catnip mice.

No matter where you put these mice in the room, the next morning they are on top or very near the food plate. It makes us wonder what the cat is thinking and why she does this.

Wildcats have a natural food-retrieving behavior for their kittens. In captivity this drive may be "discharged" inappropriately, like your cat bringing her "prey" to a particular place—not her nest, but her food plate!

After recently losing a much-loved, seemingly healthy, four-year-old Manx cat, I have learned a lot of little-known facts about feeding cats. If one were to believe the cat food commercials, to keep Morris happy and healthy, all one has to do is open a can of cat tuna, seafood treat, or whatever. Our cat, an altered male, loved these canned fishes and the dried cat foods, and this is what killed him. He got too much bone, not enough fat, and, as a result, developed kidney and bladder stones and died about ten years before he should have. I don't think many cat owners realize that a cat's diet is a complex thing—an exclusive fish diet results in a nervous disorder, too much protein aggravates the kidney problems of male cats, and most commercial cat foods don't have enough fat, etc., etc. I'd like advice on what to feed a cat, and some of the danger signals to watch for that indicate the animal is getting an improper diet. One must also avoid making the cat a finicky eater. Our new one is fed much as our children were—three meals a day (while she is still a kitten) at specific times, no snacking to speak of, and a wide variety of foods so she won't get hooked on any one. Most pet food has very complete nutritional labeling, but few people really know what nutrients a cat needs, and the harm that can result from an unbalanced diet.

Cats, dogs, and all animals need a balanced diet. Commercial feeds that consist of all fish or all beef can kill if that is all the animal is given. Researchers in England have produced thyroid, skeletal, and cardiac defects in kittens raised exclusively on an all-meat diet. Such foods should be given *only* as an occasional luxury supplement. Too often, because the owner loves his pet, he will feed it only the most expensive foods, many of which are not scientifically balanced. This kind of love kills.

Many food companies are guilty of unethical practice; having taken over the TV advertising time from the banned cigarette commercials, they tell us that if you love your pet, you will feed Product X; it's good because it's expensive and just watch how your pet will eat it up. Taste additives (fish, garlic, etc.) make the food superattractive, and very soon the pet refuses to eat his regular, less palatable, but nutritionally more complete chow. He becomes "addicted" and may develop a deficiency disease either because certain vitamins or minerals are lacking or because certain enzymes or excesses of certain elements block the absorption of essential nutrients; some, like Vitamin E, may even be destroyed in the can.

Other food companies claim that your cat (or dog) is a miniature lion (wolf)—a flesh eater, so all he needs is an all-meat diet. This is gross misinformation and is unethical and morally criminal. As pointed out earlier, an all-meat diet can kill; it can stress an old animal that has imperfect kidney functioning and may cause fatal uremia. Castrated male cats are more susceptible to develop bladder stones, and because the penis is small, these calculi can block the urethra; the bladder then becomes distended, kidneys malfunction, uremia develops, or acute shock and peritonitis when the bladder bursts. The first signs of this are straining to urinate, dribbling and licking of the genitals; when the condition is diagnosed early, veterinary intervention and medication to change the pH (acidity) of the urine to prevent further calculus formation is extremely effective.

Although many food companies claim that their product is good for all cats (or dogs) of all ages, this again is nonsense and purposefully misleading. A large, fast-growing Great Dane needs special mineral supplements to prevent rickets; a pregnant and lactating pet and her weaned offspring need more protein; an aged pet needs less protein if its kidneys are below par and a low-salt diet if it has a heart condition. Your veterinarian can help you make up the right rations or give you a prescription diet; the motto is simple—don't be sucked in by the commercials but ask your veterinarian. If he is vague, go to another vet until you are satisfied.

Commercial companies are also into the sales pitch of making the pet food look like human food—attractive, smelling nice (to our noses), full of gravy, vegetables, etc. This is an anthropomorphizing manipulation, but it is okay if the preparation is nutritionally balanced. Cats, and especially dogs, will naturally eat the most putrid or unpalatable-looking stuff to human eyes. The dry and semidry commercial chows look very unappetizing to us, but remember they are often far superior to many of the canned delicacies with which one can indulge one's pet.

Wild carnivores will often eat the stomach contents of their prey first—this consists of semi-digested plant material: yes, salad before the main meat course, and the meat course is not all meat (muscle) but includes skin, intestines, mesenteric (abdominal) fat, brain, heart, liver, and kidneys, and finally, for "dessert," bones instead of nuts and fruit. Cats, especially, eat grass and this is a good natural tonic for the cat confined to an apartment. Maintain it on a basic, balanced diet such as one of the major brands of cat chows and give it an occasional treat of canned tuna, chicken parts, or whatever—even boiled chicken scraps and kidneys are good. Your cat will become a finicky eater if it is overindulged and given too much of what it likes. If it refuses to eat its regular food after a new tasty treat, remove all food for a day or so. It is a good idea, too, for people to do what you are doing with your new kitten, namely exposing it to a variety of foods early in life. It is possible for cats and dogs to become *imprinted* onto a particular kind of food early in life and to refuse any other kind later on. (This is one of the dreams of the pet food companies—to produce the right stimulus or compound to effectively imprint or addict the pet to their product!)

I have had calls like: My pet will eat only boiled flounder and won't eat anything else; he has eczema now, what can I do? People who love their pets and overindulge them find it hard to swallow my advice, which is to get the addict unhooked—starve the pet for two, three, or more days. A hungry animal will eventually eat anything. A rare complication here is depression, and a shot of Vitamin B complex to stimulate the appetite may then be given by your veterinarian. But don't give in; your pet's life may depend on it, and love can kill.

My four-month-old kitten gets the "crazies" in the early evening, just going wild and tearing about the house. Is he abnormal and does he need a tranquilizer?

No, your cat is not abnormal, nor does he need a tranquilizer. This is just the high spirits of a healthy, playful cat. You might have fun stalking or chasing him at this playful time, and be sure to give him some fluffy toys to kill and perhaps retrieve when you throw them. In the wild, the cat would probably be most active at this time, hunting for prey, and it may well be an ancestral pattern (a "throwback" if you wish). One of my own cats used to get so excited during these evening peaks in activity that he would soon after have a bout of diarrhea. Most cats cool down as they mature, but on some evenings they will still "turn on" for a while and engage in this evening ritual.

My Persian continually gets big mats and balls of fur in her coat. How can I stop this?

Many cats, either lazy ones or those with too much fur, don't groom themselves enough and the fur will soon become matted. A sick cat will not groom itself and a cardinal sign of ill health is an unkempt-looking coat in a cat that normally kept itself well groomed. With your Persian, who is probably a lazy soul, I suggest you groom her at least once a day and cut away some of the long feathers around the hindquarters and under the belly and chest. Neatly done, it will hardly be noticeable and will save you a lot of trouble.

I bought a Siamese and it hasn't a kink in its tail. A friend says it is not a thoroughbred Siamese unless it is cross-eyed and has a kink in its tail. Why so?

Your friend is incorrect. Many Siamese do have severe, sometimes almost blinding, squints, and misalignment of the tail vertebrae is common. These are not signs of a good pedigree, although they are often mistaken for such by lay people. They are undesirable traits and are an indication of excessive inbreeding.

Cat Owners Ask Me

I swear my cat was using the tip of her tail for her kittens to play with. She lies there looking at her babies, then at the tip of her tail as she switches it to and fro. Is this really conscious or intentional? I mean, I thought animals are not aware of what they are doing.

You have made an interesting observation and the conclusion that your cat knows full well what she is doing is not an anthropomorphization. Many animals, I believe, are fully conscious of the consequence of their own actions (*i.e.,* they have insight). My Abyssinian cat will roll over onto one side as though resting, but the tip of his tail is twitching. This is the "lure" he sets for Mocha, his companion Burmese. As soon as she gets near his tail, he will suddenly grab her. Other times he will hiss, as though to put her down, and simply walk away!

Do the different breeds of cat have different personalities, and, if so, which is the best for a young single person who is out at work most of the day?

Yes, the different varieties of cats do have temperaments that tend to be fairly predictable. The Abyssinian is affectionate and even-tempered, the Burmese seductive, very playful, and usually unruffled by disruptions in the household. The Siamese can be extremely dependent, loyal, and trainable. Some tend to be flighty and extremely timid and others very unpredictable and even downright aggressive. Persians tend to be quiet, sensitive, affectionate, and enjoy the comforts of the soft life which their coats reflect; they need and enjoy a lot of attention. The "mongrel cats"—which can range from Persianlike fluffy, long-haired individuals to tiger-striped, black, or gray shorthair—cover a whole spectrum of temperaments. How much their temperament is linked with their coat type, with the way in which they are raised, and with their heritage from parents, cannot always be ascertained. Basically one can less assuredly predict what kind of personality one of these kittens will develop than with a kitten from one of the above breeds or varieties. Some will be aloof, shy, unpredictable, and moody; others "homely" and accepting and affectionate; and others downright inscrutable, appearing to always be one step ahead of the owner and all comers, dogs included! I think you would be happy with any cat, provided you choose a bright, active kitten that is outgoing and not overly timid, and provided you give it plenty of attention to socialize it as it matures.

How can I stop our kitten from playing too rough and biting and scratching?

Kittens do get carried away when they play and the best thing to do is to instigate firm discipline. Shout "no," flip it briskly on the nose, and stop playing for a while. It should quickly learn to control its bite and keep the claws retracted. Don't pull your hand away suddenly. Your cat may accidentally scratch you. And don't wear gloves for protection when you play with it. The cat would then never learn control. Young kittens will claw onto you when they are not being held securely, as will older cats when they are apprehensive. A child who does not handle a kitten competently may scare it and get scratched because the kitten reaches out with its claws for fear of falling.

People say animals have whiskers to improve their sense of touch. Is it true that a cat's whiskers help it judge the size of a hole at night so that it will know if it can get its body through?

This is the usual answer given to the possible function of the vibrissae, or whiskers, which are extremely sensitive to touch. I don't agree with it though. Many animals have whiskers even though they always live in the open and never go into tight places, while others have whiskers either much longer or shorter than their actual body width. Observing animals in the wild, we see how much they rely on the sense of smell. But how can they accurately locate the source of the smell without tracking it like a dog, nose to the ground? Simply by rapidly sensing the direction of even the faintest breeze, which carries the scent to the nose. My guess is they use the vibrissae on each side of the face as wind direction detectors, which, in combination with the sense of smell, account for the swift perception of the source of any odor. Hunters and naturalists will attest to this: If you keep "downwind" (with the wind in your face), an animal ahead may not detect you.

Notice next time how an inquisitive cat or rat twitches its whiskers as it sniffs around. Without whiskers it would be much more difficult to locate the exact source of an odor, as it is when there is no breeze or the breeze is blowing the other way.

Why do you and other people like you spend so much time and public money to make the lives of dogs and cats better? Why not do something worthwhile and help the mentally sick and retarded and poor children?

This is the kind of question I like. There's nothing like clearing the air, and for people (like me) to look where they are. A lot of animal research is simply for the sake of knowledge and has little, if any, practical value. Much of what I have written in *Understanding Your Dog* and *Understanding Your Cat* is derived from basic scientific research. It is surprising what value much dog research has when it is recast to help analyze and interpret various aspects of animal behavior. Such basic knowledge is of immense value in studying child development and abnormal behavior in human beings. It is only by comparing animals and man that we can truly understand what is going on in man.

Research on the circulation of the heart of the frog laid the foundation for comprehending the physiology of human circulation. Experimental surgery in the dog made heart surgery in man a reality today.

I, too, am concerned about priorities, and I think that much research that is done today is of lower priority than many of the problems facing humanity.

Bibliography

EWER, R. F., *The Carnivores*. Ithaca, N.Y., Cornell University Press, 1973.

FOX, M. W., "The Behavior of Cats," in E. S. E. Hafez, ed., *The Behaviour of Domestic Animals*. London, Ballière, Tindall & Cassell, 1974.

———*Understanding Your Dog*. New York, Coward, McCann & Geoghegan, 1971.

———*Behavior of Wolves, Dogs and Related Canids*. New York, Harper & Row, 1971.

LEYHAUSEN, P., *Verhaltensstudien an Katzen*. Berlin, Paul Parey, 1973.

MÉRY, F., *The Life, History and Magic of the Cat*. New York, Grosset & Dunlap, 1972.

Index

209

NOTES

NOTES

NOTES